CHURCH—CLUB—GOVERNMENT

—any organized group must run by rules which all members understand and accept. Here is a basic manual of these rules, which were used by organizations all over the world for many years.

Rachel Vixman, an experienced parliamentarian, has prepared a modern Commentary and Guide for this unique edition. It makes clear many of the complexities of the basic rules by means of easy-to-follow charts and diagrams as well as pertinent examples.

Whether as officer or member of any group, you can function more effectively with this invaluable guide to fair and efficient procedure.

ROBERT'S RULES OF ORDER

GENERAL HENRY M. ROBERT
With a
GUIDE AND COMMENTARY
by
RACHEL VIXMAN

A JOVE BOOK

Introduction, Guide and Commentary are
Copyright © 1967 by Jove Publications, Inc.

All rights reserved. No part of this publication may be reproduced or transmitted in any form or by any means, electronic or mechanical, including photocopy, recording, or any information storage and retrieval system, without permission in writing from the publisher.

Twenty-six previous printings
First Jove edition published September 1977
Fourth printing October 1980

Printed in the United States of America

Jove books are published by Jove Publications, Inc.,
200 Madison Avenue, New York, NY 10016

INTRODUCTION

ROBERT'S RULES has been a familiar guide to parliamentary procedure for almost a century. Now, somewhat modified but more authoritative than ever, these rules are widely used to govern meetings and resolve disagreement.

Robert's Rules are based primarily on parliamentary procedure originally used in the British Parliament. These procedures were subsequently brought to the New World by the early colonists and introduced at the first New England Town Meetings. When Thomas Jefferson became President of the United States, he published the first American book on parliamentary procedure in 1801. This became one of the main sources for the rules in Congress and continued to be the foremost authority on parliamentary procedure until Cushing's *Manual* was published in 1844.

It remained for Henry Martin Robert, an engineer and general in the United States Army, to modify these rules to meet the needs of "ordinary societies." His first *Robert's Rules of Order,* published in 1876, soon became a handbook for organizations, clubs and schools all over the land. In a constructive way, it exposed the uselessness of attending meetings which began late and dragged on. It gave enlightenment and comfort to frustrated members who, without knowledge, were easily victimized by overbearing chairmen and ruthless small cliques. And it armed the general membership with the know-how to combat those seeking to push through controversial resolutions without proper consideration.

Such was the widespread use of the first *Robert's Rules of Order* that General Robert published three additional books; *Robert's Rules of Order Revised,* in 1915; *Parliamentary Practice, An Introduction to Parliamentary Law,* in 1921; and *Parliamentary Law,* a reference book, in 1923. He died soon after at the age of 86.

Robert's Rules of Order provides a group guide to democratic action. But it also imposes a great responsibility on individuals to understand and master the democratic procedures so painstakingly provided. To make this more attainable, Pyramid Books has issued this newly enriched inexpensive edition, the first in paperback, with clarifying charts and diagrams and a wealth of easy-to-follow explanatory material.

The careful reading and use of this material can help guarantee orderliness and fair play in the conduct of a variety of our everyday activities.

Floyd M. Riddick

FLOYD M. RIDDICK
Parliamentarian,
United States Senate

TABLE OF CONTENTS

Table of Rules Relating to Motions	11
Preface	17
Introduction.	21
Parliamentary Law	21
Plan of the Work	23
" Part I.	24
" Part II.	25
" Part III.	25
Definitions and Common Errors	25

Part I.—Rules of Order.

Art. I.—Introduction of Business.	27
§ 1. How introduced	27
2. Obtaining the floor	27
3. What precedes debate on a question	29
4. What motions to be in writing, and how they shall be divided	30
5. Modification of a motion by mover	30
Art. II.—General Classification of Motions.	31
§ 6. Principal or Main motions	31
7. Subsidiary or Secondary motions	31
8. Incidental motions	32
9. Privileged motions	32
Art. III.—Motions and Order of Precedence.	33
Privileged Motions.	33
§ 10. To fix the time to which to adjourn	33
11. Adjourn	33
12. Questions of privilege	35
13. Orders of the day	35
Incidental Motions.	37
14. Appeal [Questions of Order]	37

15. Objection to consideration of a question	39
16. Reading papers	39
17. Withdrawal of a motion	40
18. Suspension of the Rules	40
Subsidiary Motions.	41
19. Lay on the table	41
20. Previous Question	43
21. Postpone to a certain day	47
22. Commit [or Refer]	47
23. Amend	49
24. Postpone indefinitely	51
Miscellaneous Motions.	52
25. Rescind	52
26. Renewal of a motion	52
27. Reconsideration	53

Art. IV.—Committees and Informal Action. 56
§ 28. Committees	56
29. " Form of their Reports	58
30. " Reception "	59
31. " Adoption "	60
32. Committee of the Whole	63
33. Informal consideration of a question	65

Art. V.—Debate and Decorum. 66
§ 34. Debate	66
35. Undebatable questions and those opening the main question to debate	67
36. Decorum in debate	69
37. Closing debate, methods of	70

Art. VI.—Vote. 71
§ 38. Voting, various modes of	71
39. Motions requiring more than a majority vote	75

Art. VII.—Officers and the Minutes. 77
§ 40. Chairman or President	77
41. Clerk, or Secretary, and the Minutes	80

Art. VIII.—Miscellaneous. 83
§ 42. Session	83
43. Quorum	85
44. Order of Business	86
45. Amendment of the Rules of Order, etc.	86

Part II.—Organization and Conduct of Business.

Art. IX.—Organization and Meetings. ... 88
  § 46. An Occasional or Mass Meeting. ... 88
    (a) Organization ... 88
    (b) Adoption of resolutions ... 89
    (c) Committee on " ... 90
    (d) Additional Officers ... 91
  47. A Convention or Assembly of Delegates ... 92
  48. A Permanent Society ... 93
    (a) First meeting ... 93
    (b) Second meeting ... 94
  49. Constitutions, By-Laws, Rules of Order and Standing Rules ... 96

Art. X.—Officers and Committees. ... 98
  § 50. President or Chairman ... 98
  51. Secretary, or Clerk, and the Minutes ... 100
  52. Treasurer ... 102
  53. Committees ... 104

Art. XI.—Introduction of Business. ... 105
  § 54. Introduction of Business ... 105
  § 55. Motions Classified according to their

Art. XII.—Motions. ... 106
  object ... 106
  56. To Modify or Amend. ... 108
    (a) Amend ... 108
    (b) Commit or refer ... 108
  57. To Defer Action. ... 108
    (a) Postpone to a certain time ... 108
    (b) Lay on the table ... 109
  58. To Suppress Debate. ... 109
    (a) Previous Question ... 109
    (b) An Order limiting or closing debate ... 110
  59. To Suppress the Question. ... 111
    (a) Objection to its consideration ... 111
    (b) Postpone indefinitely ... 111
    (c) Lay on the table ... 111
  60. To consider a question the second time. ... 112
    (a) Reconsider ... 112
  61. Orders and Rules ... 113
    (a) Orders of the day ... 113
    (b) Special orders ... 113

(c) Suspension of the rules	114
(d) Questions of order	114
(e) Appeal	114
62. Miscellaneous.	115
(a) Reading of papers	115
(b) Withdrawal of a motion	115
(c) Questions of privilege	115
63. To close a meeting.	115
(a) Fix the time to which to adjourn	115
(b) Adjourn	115
Art. XIII.—Miscellaneous.	116
§ 64. Debate	116
65. Forms of stating and putting questions	117

Part III.—Miscellaneous.

§ 66. Right of an Assembly to Punish its members	119
67. Right of an Assembly to Eject any one from its place of meeting	119
68. Rights of Ecclesiastical Tribunals	120
69. Trial of Members of Societies	120
70. Call of the House	122

GUIDE AND COMMENTARY by Rachel Vixman

Part One

The Rules—What They Mean and What They Do	130

Part Two

Organization Structure and Accepted Procedures	155
Bibliography	182
Diagram of Parliamentary Motions in Order of Precedence	183
Index	184

TABLE OF RULES
RELATING TO MOTIONS

12 — **ROBERT'S RULES OF ORDER**

TABLE OF RULES RELATING TO MOTIONS

Containing Answers to Two Hundred Questions in Parliamentary Practice.

NOTES

(1) Every motion in this column has the effect of suspending some rule or established right of deliberative assemblies (see note to § 39), and therefore requires a two-thirds vote, unless a special rule to the contrary is adopted.

(2) Undebatable if made when another question is before the assembly.

(3) An Amendment may be either (1) by *"adding"* or (2) by *"striking out"* words or paragraphs; or (3) by *"striking out certain words and inserting others,"* or (4) by *"substituting"* a different motion on the same subject; or (5) by *"dividing the question"* into two or more questions as specified by the mover, so as to get a separate vote on any particular point or points.

(4) An Appeal is undebatable only when relating to indecorum, or to transgressions of the rules of speaking, or to the priority

Explanation of the Table.—A Star shows that the rule heading the column in which it stands, applies to the motion opposite to which it is placed; a blank shows that the rule does not apply; a figure shows that the rule only partially applies, the figure referring to the note showing the limitations. Take, for example, "Lay on the Table;" the Table shows that § 19 of the Pocket Manual treats of this motion; that it is "undebatable" and "cannot be amended;" and that an affirmative vote on it (as shown in note 5) "cannot be reconsidered;"—the four other columns containing blanks show that this motion does not "open the main question to debate," that it does not "require a ⅔ vote," that it does "require to be seconded," and that it is not "in order when another member has the floor."

[*See page 15.*]

Section in Pocket Manual		Undebatable [§ 35].	Opens Main Question to Debate [§ 35].	Cannot be Amended [§ 23].	Cannot be Reconsidered [§ 27].	Requires a ⅔ Vote [§ 39].—See Note 1.	Does not require to be Seconded [§ 3].	In order when another has the floor [§ 2].
11	Adjourn	*			2			
10	Adjourn, Fix the Time to which to ——							
23	Amend [3]			*				
23	Amend an Amendment			*				
45	Amend the Rules	*				*		
14	Appeal, relating to indecorum, etc. [4]	*						*

RELATING TO MOTIONS

14	Appeal, all other cases	-	*	-	-	-	-	*	of business, or when made while the Previous Question is pending. When debatable, only one speech from each member is permitted. On a tie vote the decision of the Chair is sustained.
14	Call to Order	*	*	-	-	-	-	*	
37	Close Debate, motion to	-	*	*	-	-	-	-	
22	Commit or Refer	*	*	*	-	-	-	-	
34	Extend the Limits of Debate, motion to	2	*	-	*	-	-	-	(5) An affirmative vote on this motion cannot be reconsidered.
10	Fix the Time to which to Adjourn	2	*	*	*	-	-	-	
36	Leave to Continue Speaking after Indecorum	*	*	-	-	5	-	-	(6) The objection can only be made when the question is first introduced, before debate.
19	Lay on the Table	*	-	-	-	-	-	-	
37	Limit Debate, motion to	*	*	*	-	-	-	*	
15	Objection to Consideration of a Question [6]	*	*	-	-	-	-	*	
13	Orders of the Day, motion for the	7	-	-	-	-	-	*	
21	Postpone to a Certain Time	*	*	*	*	-	-	-	(7) Allows of but limited debate upon the propriety of the postponement.
24	Postpone Indefinitely	*	*	-	-	-	-	-	
20	Previous Question [8]	*	-	-	-	-	-	-	
44	Priority of Business, questions relating to	*	-	-	-	-	-	-	(8) The Previous Question, if adopted, cuts off debate and brings the assembly to a vote on the pending question only, except where the pending motion is an amendment or a motion to commit, when it also applies to the question to be amended or committed.
12	Privilege, Questions of	*	-	-	-	-	-	-	
16	Reading Papers	*	-	-	-	-	-	-	
27	Reconsider a Debatable Question	*	*	-	*	-	9	-	
27	Reconsider an Uncebatable Question	*	-	-	*	-	9	-	
22	Refer (same as Commit)	*	*	*	-	-	-	-	
25	Rescind	*	*	*	*	*	-	-	
11	Rise (in Committee equals Adjourn)	*	-	-	-	-	-	-	(9) Can be moved and entered on the record when another has the floor, but cannot interrupt business then before the assembly; must be made on the day, or the day after, the original vote was taken, and by one who voted with the prevailing side.
13	Special Order, to make a	2	*	*	-	-	-	-	
23	Substitute (same as Amend)	*	*	*	-	-	-	-	
18	Suspend the Rules	*	-	-	-	-	-	-	
19	Take from the Table	*	-	-	-	-	-	-	
44	Take up a Question out of its Proper Order	*	-	-	-	-	-	-	
17	Withdrawal of a Motion	*	-	-	-	5	-	-	

See next page for *Order of Precedence of Motions* and *Forms of Putting Certain Questions*.

ADDITIONAL RULES TO ACCOMPANY TABLE

Order of Precedence of Motions.

The ordinary motions rank as follows, and any of them (except to amend) can be made while one of a lower order is pending, but none can supersede one of a higher order; the Previous Question requires a two-thirds vote, the others only a majority:

Undebatable.
- *To Fix the Time to which to Adjourn.*
- *To Adjourn* (when unqualified) ⎫
- *For the Orders of the Day.* ⎬ Cannot be Amended.
- *To Lay on the Table.* ⎪
- *The Previous Question* (⅔ vote). ⎭

Debatable.
- *To Postpone to a Certain Time.* ⎫
- *To Commit or Refer.* ⎬ Can be Amended.
- *To Amend.* ⎪
- *To Postpone Indefinitely.* ⎭

The motion to Reconsider can be made when any other question is before the assembly, but cannot be acted upon until the business then before the assembly is disposed of [see note 9 above], when, if called up, it takes precedence of all other motions, except to adjourn, and to fix the time to which to adjourn. Questions incidental to those before the assembly, take precedence of them and must be acted upon first.

Forms of Putting Certain Questions.

If the *Previous Question* is demanded, it is put thus: "Shall the main question be now put?" or "Shall debate be now closed, and the vote taken on the pending question? [or "on the resolution?" or "amendment?"].

If an *Appeal* is made from the decision of the Chair, the question is put thus: "Shall the decision of the Chair stand as the judgment of the assembly [convention, society, etc.]?"

If the *Orders of the Day* are called for, the question is put thus: "Will the assembly now proceed to the Orders of the Day?"

When, upon the introduction of a question, some one *objects to its consideration,* the chairman immediately puts the question thus: "Will the assembly consider it?" or, "Shall the question be considered [or discussed]?"

If the vote has been ordered to be taken by *yeas and nays,* the question is put in a form similar to the following: "As many as are in favor of the adoption of these resolutions will, when their names are called, answer *yes* [or *aye*]—those opposed will answer *no.*"

REMARKS UPON THE TABLE OF RULES RELATING TO MOTIONS

The preceding Table furnishes, (1) an index to the rules relating to motions; (2) lists of the motions belonging to each of the seven classes indicated by the headings to the columns (by noticing the stars in each column); and (3) lists of the motions to which these headings in part apply, the extent to which they apply being shown in notes referred to by figures in the columns. After the Table, page 14, is a list of the most common motions, showing their order of precedence, and whether they can be amended or debated, and what vote they require—the four most important points about a motion; this list should be memorized. The peculiar form of putting certain questions is also shown. If it is desired to ascertain the proper motion to accomplish a special object, see § 55. For further information in regard to motions examine the Index under the title *Motions*.

HOW TO USE THE TABLE IN MIDST OF BUSINESS

When a motion is made, turn to the Order of Precedence of Motions, page 14, to see if it is in order. If it is in order and more information is wanted than is there furnished, look for the motion in the Table, and glance along the line to see if there are any stars in the columns. If there are no stars, then the rules at the head of the columns do not apply, and the motion is just like any resolution or amendment—that is (1) it is debatable; (2) the debate must be strictly confined to the motion; (3) it can be amended; (4) it can be reconsidered; (5) it requires a majority vote for its adoption; (6) it requires to be seconded; and (7) it is not in order when another has the floor. These general principles should be fixed in the mind and they should be strictly observed, unless a star shows that the motion is an exception to the general rule, or a figure refers to a note showing to what extent it is an exception. In this way the chairman or any other member may in a moment learn the correct rulings on all the above points.

To Illustrate—An amendment of a resolution being before the assembly, it is moved to refer it to a committee [or "to commit"]. The "Order of Precedence of Motions" shows that "to commit" is in order [because it stands above "to amend"], and the Table shows that it differs from an ordinary resolution in that it "opens to debate the main question" [that is, the original resolution]. Now if it is moved to "indefinitely postpone" the question, the chairman should rule it out of order, as he would see from a glance at the "Order of Precedence of Motions." If it is moved "to lay the question on the table," it will be found, as above, to be in order, and the table decides instantly the seven points. [See Explanation at head of Table.]

PREFACE

A work on parliamentary law has long been needed, based, in its general principles, upon the rules and practice of Congress, but adapted, in its details, to the use of ordinary societies. Such a work should not only give the methods of organizing and conducting meetings, the duties of officers and names of ordinary motions, but should also state systematically in reference to each motion, its object and effect; whether it can be amended or debated; if debatable, the extent to which it opens the main question to debate; the circumstances under which it can be made, and what other motions can be made while it is pending. This Manual has been prepared with a hope of supplying the above information in a condensed and systematic form, each rule in Part I either being complete in itself, or giving references to every section that in any way qualifies it, so that a stranger to the work can refer to any special subject with safety.

A Table of Rules is placed immediately before this Preface, which will enable a presiding officer to decide some two hundred common and important questions of parliamentary law without turning a page.

The Second Part is a simple explanation of the common methods of conducting business in ordinary meetings. The motions are classified here according to their uses, and those used for a similar purpose are compared with each other. This part is intended for that large class in every community who are almost wholly unacquainted with parliamentary usages, and are not able to devote much study to the subject, but would be glad with little labor to learn enough to enable them to take part in meetings of deliberative assemblies without fear of being out of order.

The Third Part contains some useful information, including the legal rights of assemblies, call of the house, etc.

The object of Rules of Order is to assist an assembly

to accomplish the work for which it was designed, in the best possible manner. To do this it is necessary to restrain the individual somewhat, as the right of an individual, in any community, to do what he pleases, is incompatible with the interests of the whole. Where there is no law, but every man does what is right in his own eyes, there is the least of real liberty. Experience has shown the importance of definiteness in the law; and in this country, where customs are so slightly established and the published manuals of parliamentary practice so conflicting, no society should attempt to conduct business without having adopted some work upon the subject, as the authority in all cases not covered by their own special rules.

It has been well said by one of the greatest of English writers on parliamentary law: "Whether these forms be in all cases the most rational or not is really not of so great importance. It is much more material that there should be a rule to go by, than what that rule is, that there may be a uniformity of proceeding in business, not subject to the caprice of the chairman, or captiousness of the members. It is very material that order, decency and regularity be preserved in a dignified public body."

H. M. R.

NOTE

In the twenty-three years since the first publication of this work many questions of parliamentary law arising under these rules have been referred to the author for decision. The most important of these rulings that are not readily deducible from the text, are incorporated in the editions later than the one hundred and forty-fifth thousand, generally in the form of additional notes. [See, especially, amendments, § 23.] The necessity of renewing the electrotype plates has also been taken advantage of to make a few changes, as indicated below, which are all in the direction of more close conformity to either the usage of Congress or the fundamental principles of parliamentary law.

The changes are as follows:

(a) The form of putting the question on the motion to *strike out* has been changed from the old peculiar parliamentary form to the natural form used in Congress and almost universally in this country. [§ 23.]

(b) In *filling blanks* the *smallest* sum has been given the precedence instead of the largest, to conform to the recent revision of the U.S. Senate Rules, and the practice of the House of Representatives and Parliament. [§ 23.]

(c) The time for making the motion to *Reconsider* has been extended to include the next day, provided a meeting is held thereon, to conform to the practice of the House of Representatives.

(d) The allowing the making at the same time of the motions to *reconsider* and *lay the motion to reconsider on the table,* has been stricken out as an unnecessary violation of the principle that only one motion can be made at a time.

(e) To *extend the limits of debate* has been included in the motions requiring a two-thirds vote, because it is a suspension of a rule or an order of the assembly.

INTRODUCTION

Parliamentary Law

Parliamentary Law refers originally to the customs and rules of conducting business in the English Parliament; and thence to the customs and rules of our own legislative assemblies. In England these usages of Parliament form a part of the unwritten law of the land, and in our own legislative bodies they are of authority in all cases where they do not conflict with existing rules or precedents.

But as a people we have not the respect which the English have for customs and precedents, and are always ready for such innovations as we think are improvements, and hence changes have been and are constantly being made in the *written* rules which our legislative bodies have found best to adopt. As each house adopts its own rules, it results that the two houses of the same legislature do not always agree in their practice; even in Congress the order of precedence of motions is not the same in both houses, and the Previous Question is admitted in the House of Representatives, but not in the Senate. As a consequence of this, the exact method of conducting business in any particular legislative body is to be obtained only from the Legislative Manual of that body.

The vast number of societies, political, literary, scientific, benevolent and religious, formed all over the land, though not legislative, are deliberative in character, and must have some system of conducting business, and some rules to govern their proceedings, and are necessarily subject to the common parliamentary law where it does not conflict with their own special rules. But as their knowledge of parliamentary law has been obtained from the usages in this country, rather than from the customs of Parliament, it has resulted that these societies have followed the customs of our own legislative bodies, and our people have thus been educated under a system of parliamentary law which is peculiar to this country, and yet so well established as to supersede the English parliamentary law as the common law of ordinary deliberative assemblies.

The practice of the National House of Representatives should have the same force in this country as the usages of the House of Commons have in England, in determining the general principles of the common parliamentary law of the land; but it does not follow that in every matter of detail the rules of Congress can be appealed to as the common law governing every deliberative assembly. In these matters of detail, the rules of each House of Congress are adapted to their own peculiar wants, and are of no force whatever in other assemblies. But upon all great parliamentary questions, such as what motions can be made, what is their order of precedence, which can be debated, what is their effect, etc., the common law of the land is settled by the practice of the United States House of Representatives, and not by that of the English Parliament, the United States Senate, or any other body.

While in extreme cases there is no difficulty in deciding the question as to whether the practice of Congress determines the common parliamentary law, yet between these extremes there must necessarily be a large number of doubtful cases upon which there would be great difference of opinion, and to avoid the serious difficulties always arising from a lack of definiteness in the law, every deliberative assembly should imitate our legislative bodies in adopting Rules of Order for the conduct of their business.*

---

* Where the practice of Congress differs from that of Parliament upon a material point, the common law of this country follows the practice of Congress. Thus in every American deliberative assembly having no rules for conducting business, the motion to adjourn would be decided to be undebatable, as in Congress, the English parliamentary law to the contrary notwithstanding; so if the Previous Question were negatived, the debate upon the subject would continue as in Congress, whereas in Parliament the subject would be immediately dismissed; so too, the Previous Question could be moved when there was before the assembly a motion either to amend, to commit, or to postpone definitely or indefinitely, just as in Congress, notwithstanding that, according to English parliamentary law, the Previous Question could not be moved under such circumstances.

When the rules of the two Houses of Congress conflict, the House of Representatives rules are of greater authority than those of the Senate in determining the parliamentary law of the country, just as the practice of the House of Commons, and not the House of Lords, determines the parliamentary law of England. For instance, though the Senate rules do not

Plan of the Work

This Manual is prepared to partially meet this want in deliberative assemblies that are not legislative in their character. It has been made sufficiently complete to answer for the rules of an assembly until they see fit to adopt special rules conflicting with and superseding any of its rules of detail, such as the Order of Business [§ 44], etc. Even in matters of detail the practice of Congress is followed, wherever it is not manifestly unsuited to ordinary assemblies; and in such cases, in Part I, there will be found, in a footnote, the Congressional practice. In the important matters referred to above, in which the practice of the House of Representatives settles the common parliamentary law of the country, this Manual strictly conforms to such practice.*

---

allow the motion for the Previous Question, and make the motion to postpone indefinitely take precedence of every other subsidiary motion [§ 7] except to lay on the table, yet the parliamentary law of the land follows the practice of the House of Representatives in recognizing the Previous Question as a legitimate motion, and assigning to the very lowest rank the motion to postpone indefinitely.

But in matters of detail, the rules of the House of Representatives are adapted to the peculiar wants of that body, and are of no authority in any other assembly. No one, for instance, would accept the following House of Representatives rules as common parliamentary law in this country: That the chairman, in case of disorderly conduct, would have the power to order the galleries to be cleared; that the ballot could not be used in electing the officers of an assembly; that any fifteen members would be authorized to compel the attendance of absent members and make them pay the expenses of the messengers sent after them; that all committees not appointed by the chair would have to be appointed by ballot, and if the required number were not elected by a majority vote, then a second ballot must be taken in which a plurality of votes would prevail; that each member would be limited in debate upon any question to one hour; that a day's notice must be given of the introduction of a bill, and that before its passage it must be read three times, and that without the special order of the assembly it cannot be read twice the same day. These examples are sufficient to show the absurdity of the idea that the rules of Congress in all things determine the common parliamentary law.

---

* On account of the party lines being so strictly drawn in Congress, no such thing as harmony of action is possible, and it has been found best to give a bare majority in the House of Representatives (but not in the Senate) the power to take final action upon a question without allowing of any discussion. In ordinary societies more regard should be paid to the rights of the minority, and a two-thirds vote be required, as in this Manual, for sustaining an objection to the introduction of a question, or for adopting a motion for the Previous Question, or for adopting an order closing or limiting debate. [See note to § 39 for a discussion of this question.] In this respect the policy of the Pocket Manual is a mean between those of the House and Senate. But some societies will doubtless find it advantageous to follow the practice of the House of Representatives, and others will prefer that of the Senate. It requires a majority, according to this Manual, to order the ayes and nays [§ 38], which is doubtless best in most assemblies: but in all bodies in which the members are responsible

The Manual is divided into three distinct parts, each complete in itself, and a Table of Rules [see page 12] containing a large amount of information in a tabular form, for easy reference in the midst of the business of a meeting.

Part I contains a set of Rules of Order systematically arranged, as shown in the Table of Contents. Each one of the forty-five sections is complete in itself, so that one unfamiliar with the work cannot be misled in examining any particular subject. Cross references are freely used to save repeating from other sections, and by this means the reader, without using the index, is referred to everything in the Rules of Order that has any bearing upon the subject he is investigating. The motions are arranged under the usual classes, in their order of rank, but in the Index under the word *motion* will be found an alphabetical list of all the motions generally used.

The following is stated in reference to each motion:

(1) Of what motions *it takes precedence* (that is, what motions may be pending, and yet it be in order to make and consider this motion).

(2) To what motions it *yields* (that is, what motions may be made and considered while this motion is pending).

(3) Whether it is *debatable* or not (all motions being debatable unless the contrary is stated).

(4) Whether it can be *amended* or not.

(5) In case the motion can have no subsidiary motion *applied* to it, the fact is stated [see Adjourn, § 11, for an example: the meaning is, that the particular motion, to adjourn, for example, cannot be laid on the table, postponed, committed or amended].

(6) The *effect* of the motion if adopted, whenever it could possibly be misunderstood.

(7) The *form of stating the question* when peculiar, and all other information necessary to enable one to understand the question.

---

to their constituents, a much smaller number should have this power. In Congress it requires but a one-fifth vote, and in some bodies a single member can require a vote to be taken by yeas and nays.

Any society adopting this Manual should make its rules govern them in all cases to which they are applicable, and in which they are not inconsistent with the By-Laws and Rules of Order of the society. [See § 49 for the form of a rule covering this case.] Their own rules should include all of the cases where it is desirable to vary from the rules in the Manual, and especially should provide for a Quorum [§ 43] and an Order of Business [§ 44], as suggested in these rules.

Part II is a Parliamentary Primer, giving very simple illustrations of the methods of organizing and conducting different kinds of meetings, stating the very words used by the chairman and speakers in making and putting various motions; it also gives, briefly, the duties of the officers, and forms of minutes and of reports of the treasurer and committees; it classifies the motions into eight classes according to their object, and then takes up separately each class and compares those in it, showing under what circumstances each motion should be used.

Part III consists of a few pages devoted to miscellaneous matters that should be understood by members of deliberative assemblies, such as the important but commonly misunderstood subjects of the Legal Rights of Deliberative Assemblies and Ecclesiastical Tribunals, etc.

Definitions and Common Errors

In addition to the terms defined above (*taking precedence of, yielding to* and *applying to,* see p. 24), there are other terms that are liable to be misunderstood, to which attention should be called.

Meeting and *Session.* For the distinction between these terms, see first note to § 42.

Previous Question. The effect of this much misunderstood motion is briefly stated in the eighth note to the Table of Rules, p. 13; a full explanation is given in § 20.

Substitute. This motion is one form of an amendment. The five forms of an amendment are shown in the third note to the Table of Rules, p. 12, and are more fully explained in § 23.

Shall the Question be Discussed? is a common form in some societies of stating the question on the consideration of a subject. It is very apt to convey a wrong impression of its effect, which is, if negatived, to dismiss the question for that session, as shown in § 15.

Accepting a Report, which is the same as adopting it, is confounded by many with receiving a report. [See note to § 30 for common errors in acting upon reports.]

The terms *Congress* and *H. R.,* when used in this Manual, refer to the U.S. House of Representatives.

The word *Assembly,* when occurring in forms of motions (as in an Appeal, § 14), should be replaced by the special term used to designate the particular assembly—as, for instance, "Society," or "Convention," or "Board."

PART I

RULES OF ORDER*

Art. I. Introduction of Business
[§§ 1-5.]

* If the reader's knowledge of the elementary details of parliamentary practice is not sufficient for him to understand these rules in Part I, he should, before proceeding further, read Part II, which is essentially a Parliamentary Primer. [See the first note to § 46.]

1. All business should be brought before the assembly by a motion of a member, or by the presentation of a communication to the assembly. It is not usual, however, to make a motion to receive the reports of committees [§ 30] or communications to the assembly; and in many other cases in the ordinary routine of business, the formality of a motion is dispensed with; but should any member object, a regular motion becomes necessary.

2. Before a member can make a motion or address the assembly upon any question, it is necessary that he *obtain the floor;* that is, he must rise and address the presiding officer by his title, thus: "Mr. Chairman," who will then announce the member's name.* Where two or more rise at the same time, the chairman must decide who is entitled to the floor, which he does by announcing that member's name. In making his decision he should be guided by the following principles:

(*a*) The member upon whose motion the subject under discussion was brought before the assembly (or, in case of a committee's report, the one who presented the report), is entitled to be recognized as having the floor (if he has not already had it during that discussion)

---

* If the chairman has some other title, as President, Moderator, etc., he is addressed by his special title, thus: "Mr. President." [See § 34.] If the chairman rises to speak before the floor has been assigned to any one, it is the duty of a member who may have previously risen to taken his seat. [See Decorum in Debate, § 36.]

27

notwithstanding another member may have first risen and addressed the chair. *(b)* No member who has once had the floor is again entitled to it while the same question is before the assembly, provided the floor is claimed by one who has not spoken to that question.* *(c)* As the interests of the assembly are best subserved by allowing the floor to alternate between the friends and enemies of a measure, the chairman, when he knows which side of a question is taken by each claimant of the floor, and their claim is not determined by the above principles, should give the preference to the one opposed to the last speaker.

From this decision of the chairman any two members can make an appeal [§ 14].† Where there is doubt as to who is entitled to the floor, the chairman can at the first allow the assembly to decide the question by a vote—the one getting the largest vote being entitled to the floor.

After the floor has been assigned to a member he cannot be interrupted by calls for the question,‡ or by a motion to adjourn, or for any purpose, by either the chairman or any member, except *(a)* to have entered on the minutes a motion to reconsider [§ 27]; *(b)* by a question of order [§ 14]; *(c)* by an objection to the consideration of the question [§ 15]; *(d)* by a call for the orders of the day [§ 13],** or *(e)* by a question of privilege that requires immediate action, as shown in § 12.

In such cases the member, when he rises and addresses the chair, should state at once for what purpose he rises, as, for instance, that he "rises to a point of order."

NOTE ON OBTAINING THE FLOOR—The chair should not recognize a member who has risen and remained standing while another member is speaking, provided anyone else rises after the speaker has yielded the floor.

---

* See § 26 for an explanation of what is necessary to technically change the question before the assembly.

† In the U.S. House of Representatives there is no appeal from the decision of the chair as to who is entitled to the floor, nor should there be any appeal in such cases in large assemblies, especially in mass meetings, as the best interests of the assembly require the chair to be given more power in such large bodies.

‡ It is a plain breach of order when a member has the floor for any one to call for the question or an adjournment; and the chairman should protect the speaker in his right to address the assembly.

** See close of first note § 13.

When a member obtains the floor and makes a debatable motion that is in order, if it is not immediately seconded, the chair should inquire if the motion is seconded (which can be done by any member, without rising or addressing the chair, simply saying, "I second it"), and the maker of the motion should then be regarded as having the refusal of the floor in preference to all other members. No motion made after his should be recognized until the chair has given ample time for members to respond to the invitation for a second, and if the motion is seconded, until after the maker of the motion has had an opportunity to claim the floor. Motions to adjourn and to lay on the table are frequently made by persons who have not the floor, and after another motion has been made, and while the maker of the latter motion is entitled to the floor. The chair should not recognize such motions.

A member submitting a report of a committee, or offering a resolution, does not lose the floor by requesting the Secretary to read the report or resolution, and the Secretary has not obtained the floor thereby, nor can the chair entertain a motion made by him, unless the member expressly yields the floor for the motion. As soon as the reading is finished the member who submits the report resumes the floor and moves its adoption, when the chair, after stating the question, recognizes the gentleman as having the floor. Of course motions that are in order when another has the floor could interrupt the member at any time.

3. Before any subject is open to debate [§ 34] it is necessary, first, that a motion be made by a member who has the floor; second, that it be seconded (see exceptions below); and third, that it be stated by the presiding officer.* When the motion is in writing it shall be handed to the chairman, and read before it is debated.

This does not prevent suggestions of alterations, before the question is stated by the presiding officer. To the contrary, much time may be saved by such informal remarks; which, however, must never be allowed to run into debate. The member who offers the motion, until it has been stated by the presiding officer, can modify his motion, or even withdraw it entirely; after it is stated he can do neither without the consent of the assembly [see §§ 5, 17]. When the mover modifies his motion, the one who seconded it can withdraw his second.

---

* Examples of the various forms of making motions are given in §§ 46, 54. Forms of stating questions will be found in § 65. Any member can second any motion from his seat without rising or addressing the chair. In Congress, motions are not required to be seconded.

Exceptions: A call for the orders of the day, a question of order (though not an appeal), or an objection to the consideration of the question [§§ 13, 14, 15], does not have to be seconded; and many questions of routine are not seconded or even made; the presiding officer merely announcing that, if no objection is made, such will be considered the action of the assembly.

4. All Principal Motions [§ 6], Amendments and Instructions to Committees, should be in writing, if required by the presiding officer. Although a question is complicated, and capable of being made into several questions, no one member (unless there is a special rule allowing it) can insist upon its being divided; his resource is to move that the question be divided, specifying in his motion how it is to be divided. Anyone else can move as an amendment to this, to divide it differently.

This *Division of a Question* is really an amendment [§ 23], and subject to the same rules. Instead of moving a division of the question, the same result can be usually attained by moving some other form of an amendment. When the question is divided, each separate question must be a proper one for the assembly to act upon, even if none of the others were adopted. Thus, a motion to "commit with instructions" is indivisible; because, if divided, and the motion to commit should fail, then the other motion to instruct the committee would be improper, as there would be no committee to instruct.* The motion to "strike out certain words and insert others" is indivisible, as it is strictly one proposition.

5. After a question has been stated by the presiding officer, it is in the possession of the assembly for debate; the mover cannot withdraw or modify it, if anyone ob-

---

* The 46th Rule of the House of Representatives requires the division of a question on the demand of one member, provided "it comprehends propositions in substance so distinct that one being taken away, a substantive proposition shall remain for the decision of the House." But this does not allow a division so as to have a vote on separate items or names. The 121st Rule expressly provides that on the demand of one-fifth of the members a separate vote shall be taken on such items separately, and others collectively, as shall be specified in the call, in the case of a bill making appropriations for internal improvements. But this right to divide a question into items extends to no case but the one specified. The common parliamentary law allows of no division except when the assembly orders it, and in ordinary assemblies this rule will be found to give less trouble than the Congressional one.

jects, except by obtaining leave from the assembly [§ 17], or by moving an amendment.*

Art. II. General Classification of Motions†
[§§ 6-9.]

† In § 54, the ordinary motions will be found classified according to their object.

6. A Principal or Main Question or Motion‡ is a motion made to bring before the assembly, for its consideration, any particular subject. No Principal Motion can be made when any other question is before the assembly. It takes precedence of nothing, and yields to all Privileged, Incidental and Subsidiary Questions [§§ 7, 8, 9].

7. Subsidiary or Secondary Motions are such as are applied to other motions, for the purpose of most appropriately disposing of them.** They take precedence of a Principal Question, and must be decided before the Principal Question can be acted upon. They yield to Privileged and Incidental Questions, [§§ 8, 9,] and are as follows (being arranged in their order of precedence among themselves):

Lay on the Table	See § 19
The Previous Question	" § 20
Postpone to a Certain Day	" § 21
Commit, or Refer, or Re-Commit	" § 22
Amend	" § 23
Postpone Indefinitely	" § 24

---

* Rule 40 H. R. is as follows: "After a motion is stated by the Speaker, or read by the Clerk, it shall be deemed to be in the possession of the House, but it may be withdrawn at any time before a decision or amendment." The practice under this rule has been, not to allow a motion to be withdrawn after the previous question has been seconded. This manual conforms to the old parliamentary principle, which is probably better adapted to ordinary societies. In certain organizations it will, doubtless, be found advisable to adopt a special rule like the Congressional one just given.

‡ No motion is in order that conflicts with the Constitution, By-Laws, or Standing Orders or Resolutions of the assembly, or any resolution already adopted during the session [§ 42], and if adopted it is null and void. In order to introduce such a motion it is necessary to amend the Constitution or By-Laws, or to rescind the rule or resolution [§ 25]. To reconsider is not a principal motion.

** Take, for example, a motion that an appeal lay on the table: to lay on the table is a subsidiary motion enabling the assembly to properly dispose of the appeal; while the appeal is an incidental question, arising out of a decision of the chair, to which some members objected.

Any of these motions (except to Amend) can be made when one of a lower order is pending, but none can supersede one of a higher order. They cannot be applied* to one another except in the following cases: *(a)* the Previous Question applies to the motions to Postpone, without affecting the principal motion, and can, if specified, be applied to a pending amendment [§ 20]; *(b)* the motions to Postpone to a certain day, to Commit and to Amend, can be amended; and *(c)* a motion to Amend the minutes can be laid on the table without carrying the minutes with it [§ 19].

8. Incidental Questions are such as arise out of other questions, and, consequently take precedence of, and are to be decided before, the questions which give rise to them. They yield to Privileged Questions [§ 9] and cannot be amended. Excepting an Appeal they are undebatable; an Appeal is debatable or not, according to circumstances, as shown in §14. They are as follows:

Appeal (or Questions of Order)	See	§ 14
Objection to the Consideration of a Question	"	§ 15
The Reading of Papers	"	§ 16
Leave to Withdraw a Motion	"	§ 17
Suspension of the Rules	"	§ 18

9. Privileged Questions are such as, on account of their importance, take precedence of all other questions whatever, and on account of this very privilege they are undebatable [§ 35], excepting when relating to the rights of the assembly or its members, as otherwise they could be made use of so as to seriously interrupt business. They are as follows (being arranged in their order of precedence among themselves):

To Fix the time to which the Assembly shall Adjourn	See	§ 10
Adjourn	"	§ 11
Questions relating to the Rights and Privileges of the Assembly or any of its Members	"	§12
Call for the Orders of the Day	"	§13

---

* See page 24 for explanation of some of these technical terms.

Art. III Motions and their Order of Precedence*
[§§ 10-27.]

Privileged Motions
[§§ 10-13; see § 9.]

10. To fix the time to which the Assembly shall Adjourn. This motion takes precedence of all others, and is in order even after the assembly has voted to adjourn, provided the chairman has not announced the result of the vote. If made when another question is before the assembly, it is undebatable [§ 35]; it can be amended by altering the time. If made when no other question is before the assembly, it stands as any other principal motion, and is debatable.† The *Form* of this motion is, "When this assembly adjourns, it adjourns to meet at such a time."

11. To Adjourn. This motion (when unqualified) takes precedence of all others, except to "fix the time to which to adjourn," to which it yields. It is not debatable, it cannot be amended or have any other subsidiary motion [§ 7] applied to it; nor can a vote on it be reconsidered. If qualified in any way, it loses its privileged character, and stands as any other principal motion. The motion to adjourn can be repeated if there has been any intervening business, though it be simply progress in debate [§ 26]).‡ When a committee is through with any business referred to it, and prepared to report, instead of adjourning, a motion should be made "to rise," which motion, committee, has the same privileges as to adjourn in the assembly [§ 32].

The *Effect upon Unfinished Business* of an adjournment is as follows** [see Session, § 42.]:

(a) When it does not close the session, the business interrupted by the adjournment is the first in order

---

* For a list of all the ordinary motions, arranged in their order of precedence, see the Table of Rules, page 10. All the Privileged and Subsidiary ones in this article are so arranged.

† In ordinary societies it is better to follow the common parliamentary law, and permit this question to be introduced as a principal question, when it can be debated and suppressed [§§ 58, 59] like other questions. In Congress it is never debatable, and has entirely superseded the unprivileged and inferior motion to "adjourn to a particular time."

‡ See Note at close of this Section.

** "After six days from the commencement of a second or subsequent session of any Congress, all bills, resolutions and reports which originated in the House, and at the close of the next preceding session remained undetermined, shall be resumed, and acted on in the same manner as if an after the reading of the minutes at the next meeting, and is treated the same as if there had been no adjournment;* an adjourned meeting being legally the continuation of the meeting of which it is an adjournment.

(b) When it closes a session in an assembly which has more than one regular session each year, then the unfinished business shall be taken up at the next succeeding session previous to new business, and treated the same as if there had been no adjournment [see § 44 for its place in the order of business]. Provided that, in a body elected for a definite time (as a board of directors elected for one year), unfinished business shall fall to the ground with the expiration of the term for which the board or any portion of them were elected.

(c) When the adjournment closes a session in an assembly which does not meet more frequently than once a year, or when the assembly is an elective body, and this session ends the term of a portion of the members, the adjournment shall put an end to all business unfinished at the close of the session. The business can be introduced at the next session, the same as if it had never been before the assembly.

NOTE ON ADJOURNMENT.—The motion to adjourn cannot be made when another has the floor, nor after a question has been put and the assembly is engaged in voting, but it is in order after the vote has been taken and before it has been announced. In this latter case when the business is resumed, the vote should be announced. In some societies a great deal of time is consumed in counting the ballots at the annual elections, and in such cases it would often be advantageous to take a short recess, or else transact other business until the tellers are ready to report. A motion could be made, "That when we adjourn, we adjourn to meet at the call of the chair," and then when this is adopted the society could adjourn, the chair calling the society to order as soon as the ballots are counted. Or, the object could be accomplished by voting to take a *Recess* of, say, fifteen minutes, which is equivalent to the above two motions, and would be in order at any time except when either of them is pending. A

---

adjournment had not taken place."—Rule 136 H. R. But unfinished business does not go over from one Congress to another Congress. Any ordinary society that meets as seldom as once a year, is apt to be composed of as different membership at its successive meetings as any two successive Congresses, and only trouble would result from allowing unfinished business to hold over to the next yearly meeting.

* Of course the assembly may adopt rules that modify this general rule, as in the case of the motion to Reconsider [§ 27] in these rules.

Recess is an adjournment of the assembly for a limited time during its session.

The assembly may vote down the motion to adjourn in order to hear one speech or take one vote, and, therefore, it must have the privilege of being renewed when there has been any progress in the business or the debate. But the chair should not allow this high privilege to be abused to the annoyance of the assembly, and therefore, should refuse to entertain the motion to adjourn when the assembly has just voted it down, and nothing has occurred since to show the assembly has any wish to adjourn.

No Appeal or Questions of Order should be entertained after the motion to adjourn has been made, unless the assembly refuses to adjourn, when they would be in order.

12. Questions of Privilege.* Questions relating to the rights and privileges of the assembly, or any of its members, take precedence of all other questions, except the two preceding, to which they yield. If the question is one requiring immediate action it can interrupt a member's speech. When such a question is raised the chairman decides whether it is a question of privilege or not, from which decision an appeal [§ 14] can be taken by any two members.

It is not necessary that the assembly take final action upon the question of privilege when it is raised—it may be referred to a committee [§ 22], or laid on the table [§ 19], or it may have any other subsidiary [§7] motion applied to it, and in such case the subsidiary motion is exhausted on it without affecting the question interrupted by the question of privilege. As soon as the latter is disposed of, the assembly resumes the consideration of the question which it interrupted.

13. Orders of the Day. A call for the Orders of the Day takes precedence of every other motion, excepting to Reconsider [§ 27], and the three preceding, to which latter three it yields, and is not debatable, nor can it be amended. It does not require to be seconded, and it is in order when another member has the floor.†

---

* Questions of Privilege must not be confounded with Privileged Questions; the latter include the former, and several other questions as shown in § 9. Disorder in the gallery, one member opening a window so as to cause a draft, endangering the health of others, charges made against the official character of a member, etc., are examples of questions of privilege.

† Rule 54 H.R. provides that at the close of the morning hour (which is devoted to reports from committees and resolutions) a motion is in order to proceed to "the business on the Speaker's table, and to the orders of the day;" it then specifies the order in which the business on the Speaker's

When one or more subjects have been assigned to a particular day or hour, they become the Orders of the Day for that day or hour, and they cannot be considered before that time, except by a two-thirds vote [§ 39]. And when that day or hour arrives, if called up, they take precedence of all but the three preceding questions [§§ 10, 11, 12] and a reconsideration [§ 27]. Instead of considering them, the assembly may appoint another time for their consideration. If not taken up on the day specified, the order falls to the ground.

The orders of the day are divided into two classes, Special Orders and General Orders, the first class always taking precedence of the latter. *General Orders* can be made by a majority, by postponing questions to certain times, or by adopting a programme or order of business for the day or session; these General Orders cannot interfere with the established rules of the assembly. A *Special Order* suspends all the rules of the assembly that interfere with its consideration at the times specified,* and it therefore requires a two-thirds vote to make any question a Special Order. This motion is in order whenever a motion to Suspend the Rules [§ 18] is in order. After one Special Order is made for a certain time, it is not in order to make another Special Order to precede or interfere with it, but a Special Order can interfere with General Orders.

When the Orders of the Day are taken up, it is necessary to take up first the Special Orders, if there are any, and then the General Orders; in each class the separate questions must be taken up in their exact order, the one first assigned to the day or hour taking precedence of one afterwards assigned to the same day or hour. (A motion to take up a particular part of the Orders of the Day, or a certain question, is not a privi-

---

table shall be considered, and closes thus: "The messages, communications and bills on his table having been disposed of, the Speaker shall then proceed to call the orders of the day." While in Congress it is not in order to interrupt a member to call for the orders of the day, yet it is the practice to permit a member, at the close of the morning hour, even though another member has the floor, to move to proceed to "the business on the Speaker's table, and to the orders of the day." To apply the above principle to ordinary assemblies, it is necessary to allow a motion for the orders of the day to interrupt a member who may have the floor, after the time has arrived for their consideration.

* Thus, if an assembly had a rule like that in § 44 for the order of business, when the time appointed for the Special Order arrived, any one could call for the Special Orders, even though a Committee were reporting at the time; but the orders for the day in general could not be called for until all the Committees' reports had been acted upon.

leged motion.) Any of the subjects, when taken up, instead of being then considered, can be assigned to some other time, a majority being competent to postpone even a Special Order.

The *Form* of this question, as put by the chair when the proper time arrives, or on the call of a member, is, "Shall the Orders of the Day be taken up?" or, "Will the assembly now proceed to the Orders of the Day?"

The *Effect* of an *affirmative vote,* on a call for the Orders of the Day, is to remove the question under consideration from before the assembly, the same as if it had been interrupted by an adjournment [§ 11].

The *Effect* of a *negative vote* is to dispense with the orders merely so far as they interfere with the consideration of the question then before the assembly.

A common case of Orders of the Day is where an assembly has adopted an order of business for the day, specifying the hour at which each question shall be considered. When the hour appointed for taking up the second question has arrived, the chairman should announce that fact, and, if no one objects, immediately put to vote the questions before the assembly, and state the question next to be considered. Should any member object to this, the chairman should at once submit to the assembly a question like this: "Will the assembly now proceed to consider [here state the subject], which was assigned to this hour?" While a programme, as here supposed, does not state the fact, yet its very form implies that at the expiration of the time allowed any subject, all the questions then pending shall be put to vote. Still, as it takes a formal vote, except by unanimous consent, to proceed originally to the Orders of the Day, so a formal vote is necessary if anyone objects to take up the next order, and close discussion on the one pending.

Incidental Motions
[§§ 14-18; see § 8.]

14. Appeal [Questions of Order].* A Question of Order takes precedence of the question giving rise to it, and must be decided by the presiding officer without debate. If a member objects to the decision, he says, "I

---

* A motion cannot be ruled out of order after it has been entertained and debated without objection. An appeal can be made only at the time of the decision of the chair.

appeal from the decision of the chair." If the appeal is seconded, the chairman immediately states the question as follows: "Shall the decision of the chair stand as the judgment of the assembly?"* If there is a tie vote the decision of the chair is sustained.

This appeal yields to Privileged Questions [§ 9]. It cannot be amended; it cannot be debated when it relates simply to indecorum [§ 36], or to transgressions of the rules of speaking, or to the priority of business, or if it is made while the previous question [§ 20] is pending. When debatable, no member is allowed to speak but once, and whether debatable or not, the presiding officer, without leaving the chair, can state the reasons upon which he bases his decision. The motion to Lay on the Table† [§ 19], and the Previous Question [§ 20] if the appeal is debatable, can be applied to an appeal, and when adopted they affect nothing but the appeal. The vote on an appeal may also be reconsidered [§ 27]. An appeal is not in order when another appeal is pending.

It is the duty of the presiding officer to enforce the rules and orders of the assembly, without debate or delay. It is also the right of every member, who notices a breach of a rule, to insist upon its enforcement. In such case he shall rise from his seat, and say, "Mr. Chairman, I rise to a point of order." The speaker should immediately take his seat, and the chairman requests the member to state his point of order, which he does, and resumes his seat. The chair decides the point, and then, if no appeal is taken, permits the first member to resume his speech. If the member's remarks are decided to be improper, and anyone objects to his continuing his speech, he cannot continue it without a vote of the assembly to that effect.

Instead of the method just described, it is usual, when it is simply a case of improper language used in debate, for a member to say, "I call the gentleman to order;" the chairman decides whether the speaker is in or out of order, and proceeds as before. The chairman can ask the advice of members when he has to decide questions

---

* The word Assembly can be replaced by Society, Convention, Board, etc., according to the name of the organization. See § 65 for a fuller explanation of the method of stating the question on an Appeal.

† In Congress, the usual course in case of an Appeal is to lay it on the table, as this practically kills it and sustains the chair.

of order, but the advice must be given sitting, to avoid the appearance of debate; or the chair, when unable to decide the question, may at once submit it to the assembly.

15. Objection to the Consideration of a Question. An objection can be made to the consideration of any principal motion [§ 6], but only when it is first introduced, before it has been debated. It is similar to a question of order [§ 14], in that it can be made while another member has the floor, and does not require a second; and as the chairman can call a member to order, so can he put this question, if he deems it necessary, upon his own responsibility. It cannot be debated [§ 35], or amended [§ 23], or have any other subsidiary motion [§ 7] applied to it. When a motion is made and any member "objects to its consideration," the chairman shall immediately put the question, "Will the assembly consider it?" or, "Shall the question be considered [or discussed]?" If decided in the negative by a two-thirds vote [§ 39], the whole matter is dismissed for that session [§ 42]; otherwise the discussion continues as if this question had never been made.

The *Object* of this motion is not to cut off debate (for which other motions are provided, see § 37), but to enable the assembly to avoid altogether any question which it may deem irrelevant, unprofitable or contentious.*

16. Reading Papers. [For the order of precedence, see § 8.] Where papers are laid before the assembly, every member has a right to have them once read before he can be compelled to vote on them, and whenever a member asks for the reading of any such paper evidently for information, and not for delay, the chair should direct it to be read, if no one objects. But a member has not the right to have anything read (excepting as stated above) without getting permission from the assembly.

---

* In Congress, the introduction of such questions could be temporarily prevented by a majority vote under the 41st Rule of the House of Representatives, which is as follows: "Where any motion or proposition is made, the question, 'Will the House now consider it?' shall not be put unless it is demanded by some member, or is deemed necessary by the Speaker." [See note at close of § 39.] The English use the "Previous Ques-

The question upon granting such permission cannot be debated or amended.

17. Withdrawal of a Motion. [For order of precedence, see §8.] When a question is before the assembly and the mover wishes to withdraw or modify it, or substitute a different one in its place, if no one objects, the presiding officer grants the permission; if any objection is made, it will be necessary to obtain leave to withdraw,* etc., on a motion for that purpose. This motion cannot be debated or amended. When a motion is withdrawn, the effect is the same as if it had never been made.

18. Suspension of the Rules.† [For the order of precedence, see § 8.] This motion is not debatable, and cannot be amended, nor can any subsidiary [§ 7] motion be applied to it, nor a vote on it be reconsidered [§ 27], nor a motion to suspend the rule for the same purpose be renewed [§ 26] at the same meeting, though it may be renewed after an adjournment, though the next meeting be held the same day.‡ The rules of the assembly shall not be suspended except for a definite purpose, and by a two-thirds vote; nor shall any rule be suspended, unless by unanimous consent, that gives any right to a minority as small as one-third.**

---

tion" for a similar purpose [see note at close of § 20].

The question of consideration is seldom raised in Congress, but in assemblies with very short sessions, where but few questions can or should be considered, it seems a necessity that two-thirds of the assembly should be able to instantly throw out a question they do not wish to consider. A very common form, in ordinary societies, of putting this question, is, "Shall the question be discussed?" The form to which preference is given in the rule conforms more to the Congressional one, and is less liable to be misunderstood.

* In Congress, a motion may be withdrawn by the mover, before a decision or amendment [Rule 40 H. R.]. Nothing would be gained in ordinary societies by varying from the old common law as stated above [see note to § 5].

† This motion applies only to Rules of Order or Standing Rules [§ 49, note], as the Constitution and By-Laws cannot be suspended even by unanimous consent, unless they provide for their own suspension, which should never be done except in case of a particular by-law relating to the transaction of business, and then it should be specified.

‡ In Congress it cannot be renewed the same day.

** There would be no use in a rule allowing one-fifth of the members present to order the yeas and nays, for instance, if two-thirds of those present could suspend the rule [see the last notes to §§ 38, 39].

MOTIONS AND ORDER OF PRECEDENCE 41

The *Form* of this motion is, "to suspend the rules which interfere with," etc., specifying the object of the suspension.

Subsidiary Motions
[§§ 19-24; see§ 7.]

19. To Lay on the Table.* This motion takes precedence of all other Subsidiary Questions [§ 7], and yields to any Privileged [§ 9] or Incidental [§ 8] Question. It is not debatable, and cannot be amended or have any other subsidiary motion [§ 7] applied to it, nor can an affirmative vote on it be reconsidered [§ 27]. It removes the subject from consideration till the assembly vote to take it from the table.

The *Form*‡ of this motion is, "I move to lay the question on the table," or, "that it be laid on the table," or, "that the question lie on the table." When it is desired to take the question up again, a motion is made, either to *take the question from the table,*† or "to now consider such and such a question;" which motion has no privilege and is undebatable, and cannot have any subsidiary motion applied to it.

The *Object* of this motion is to postpone the subject in such a way that it can be taken up at any time, either at the same or some future meeting, which could not be accomplished by a motion to postpone, either definitely or indefinitely. It is also frequently used to suppress a question [§ 59] for the session, which it does, provided a majority vote can never be obtained to take it from the table during that session [§ 42].

The *Effect* of this motion** is in general to place on the table for that entire session [§ 42] everything that adheres to the subject; so that if an amendment be ordered to lie on the table, the subject which it is proposed to amend goes there with it. The following cases

---

* See Note at close of this Section.

‡ A motion to lay a question on the table for a specified time should not be ruled out of order but should be recognized and stated by the chair as a motion to postpone to a definite time. The motion to lay on the table cannot be limited in any way.

† In organizations whose sessions do not last longer than a day, and are as frequent as monthly, it should be allowed to take from the table any question laid on the table at the previous session [§ 42]. With a resolution it would generally be better to offer it anew.

** A question of privilege [§ 12] does not adhere to the subject it may happen to interrupt, and consequently if laid on the table does not carry with it the question pending when it was raised.

are exceptional: (*a*) An appeal [§ 14] being laid on the table, has the effect of sustaining, at least for the time, the decision of the chair, and does not carry the original subject to the table. (*b*) So when a motion to reconsider [§ 27] a question is laid on the table, the original question is left just where it was before the reconsideration was moved. (*c*) An amendment to the minutes being laid on the table does not carry the minutes with it.

Even after the ordering of the Previous Question up to the moment of taking the last vote under it, it is in order to lay upon the table the questions still before the assembly.

NOTE ON LAYING ON THE TABLE.—This motion has high privileges, outranking every debatable question, and being undebatable itself and requiring only a majority vote for its adoption, because it is for the best interests of the assembly that it have the power to instantly lay aside any business to attend to something more urgent. The fundamental principles of parliamentary law require that every motion which suppresses a question for the session should be open to free debate [note at close of § 35], unless debate is limited or closed by at least a two-thirds vote [note at close of § 39]. In assemblies having short sessions lasting for only a few hours, a bare majority can lay on the table every objectionable question and thus suppress it without permitting debate. This is an abuse of the motion that often interferes with the harmony of voluntary organizations. The reasons for giving it such high privileges are based on the theory that the question is to be laid aside only temporarily. The motion is very valuable if used for its legitimate purpose, but if used habitually to suppress questions, then it should require a two-thirds vote.

The minority has no remedy for the unfair use of this motion, but the evil could be slightly diminished as follows: The person who introduces a resolution is sometimes cut off from speaking by the motion to lay the question on the table being made as soon as the chair states the question, or even before. In such cases the introducer of the resolution should always claim the floor, to which he is entitled [note at close of § 2], and make his speech. Persons are commonly in such a hurry to make this motion that they neglect to address the chair and obtain the floor. In such case one of the minority should address the chair quickly, and, if not given the floor, make the point of order that he is the first one to address the chair and that the other member not having the floor was not entitled to make a motion.

As motions laid on the table are merely temporarily laid aside, the majority should remember that the minority may all stay to the moment of final adjournment and then be in the majority and take up and pass the resolutions laid on the table. The safer and fairer method is to object to the consideration of the question [§ 15] if it is so objectionable that it is not desired to allow even its introducer to speak on it; or if there has been debate so it cannot be objected to, then move the Previous Question, which, if adopted, immediately brings the assembly to a vote. These are legitimate motions for getting at the sense of the members at once as to whether they wish the subject discussed, and as they require a two-thirds vote for their adoption, no one has a right to object to their being made.

This motion, to lay on the table, cannot be applied to more than the question then before the meeting and whatever necessarily adheres to it. Thus, it is improper to lay on the table "Reports of Committees," or "Unfinished Business," when they are reached in the order of business. The object sought by such motions can only be attained by "suspending the rules" [18], which requires a two-thirds vote, or by laying on the table each successive report as it comes up for action.

20. The Previous Question* takes precedence of every debatable question [§ 35], and yields to Privileged [§ 9] and Incidental [§ 8] Questions, and to the motion to Lay on the Table [§ 19]; and after the demand for the previous question up to the time of taking final action under it, it is in order to move an adjournment or that the main question be laid on the table. It is not debatable, and cannot be amended or have any other subsidiary [§ 7] motion applied to it. It applies to questions of privilege [§ 12] as well as to any other debatable questions. It is allowable for a member to submit a resolution and at the same time move the previous question thereon. It may be reconsidered,† but not after

---

* The Previous Question is a technical name for this motion, conveying a wrong impression of its import, as it has nothing to do with the subject previously under consideration. To demand the previous question is equivalent in effect to moving "That debate now cease, and the assembly immediately proceed to vote on the pending question" [or "questions" in some cases, as shown above under the *effect* of the previous question]. So when the chairman puts the question, "Shall the main question be now put?" it means "Shall the pending question be now put?" [or "questions," as just stated]. The origin of this question, and the changes that have taken place in its effects, are described in the note at the close of this section. See § 37 for the motion to *Limit Debate*.

† Usually but a single vote is taken in reconsidering the previous question, thus: "Will the assembly reconsider the motion ordering the previous question?" If decided affirmatively the question is divested of the previous question. This is reasonable, as the previous question is undebatable and cuts off debate, and therefore no one would vote to reconsider

it is partly executed. It shall require a two-thirds* vote for its adoption.

When a member calls for the previous question, and the call is seconded, the presiding officer must immediately put the question, "Shall the main question be now put?" If it fails, the discussion continues as if this motion had not been made.

If adopted, its *Effect* is as follows: [See the illustration near the close of this section].

(1) Its effect [excepting when to Amend or to Commit is pending] is to instantly close debate,† and bring the assembly to a vote upon the pending question. This vote being taken, the effect of the previous question is exhausted, and the business before the assembly stands exactly as if the vote on the pending motion had been taken in the usual way, without having been forced to it by the previous question; so if this vote is reconsidered [§ 27] the question is divested of the previous question, and is again open to debate.

(2) Its effect when either of the motions to Amend [§ 23] or to Commit [§ 22] is pending, is to cut off debate, and to force a vote, not only upon the motions to amend and to commit, but also upon the question to be amended or committed.‡ The chairman puts to vote all these questions in their order of precedence, beginning with the one last moved [see illustrations further on]. The previous question is not exhausted until votes have been taken on all these questions, or else it has been voted to refer the subject to a committee. If one of these votes is reconsidered before the previous question is exhausted, the pendency of the previous question precludes debate upon the motion reconsidered.

---

it who is not in favor of re-opening the debate.

* In the House of Representatives it must be seconded by a majority [to avoid the yeas and nays], and then it can be adopted by a majority vote; in the U.S. Senate it is not allowed. It is sometimes called the "gag law," which name is deserved when a bare majority can adopt it. The right of debate should be considered as an established rule of every deliberative assembly, which cannot be interfered with excepting by a vote that is competent to suspend any other rule. [See note to § 39.]

† After debate is closed upon a question which has been reported from a committee, the member reporting the measure has the right to make the closing speech. [See § 34.]

‡ If we consider the motion to amend and to commit as inseparably connected with the question to be amended or committed, so that together they constitute but one question, then it would be correct to say that the only effect of adopting the Previous Question is to cut off debate and to force the assembly to vote upon the *one question pending*. This will to

The motion for the previous question may be limited to the pending amendment, and if adopted, debate is closed on the amendment only. After the amendment is voted on, the main question is again open to debate and amendment. [In this case the form of the question would be similar to this, "Shall the question be now put on the amendment?"*] So in the same manner it can be moved on an amendment of an amendment.

The *Object* of the previous question is to bring the assembly to a vote on the question before it without further debate.†

An Appeal [§ 14] from the decision of the chair is undebatable [§ 35] if made after the previous question has been moved, and before final action has been taken under it.

To *Illustrate the Effect* of the previous question under all kinds of circumstances, take the following examples:

(*a*) Suppose a question is before the assembly, and an amendment to it offered, and then it is moved to postpone [§ 21] the question to another time: the previous question now being ordered stops the debate and forces a vote on the pending question—the postponement. When that vote is taken the effect of the previous question is exhausted. If the assembly refuses to postpone the subject, the debate is resumed upon the pending amendment.

(*b*) Suppose the subject under consideration is interrupted by a question of privilege [§ 12], and it has been moved to refer this latter question to a committee: the previous question being now ordered brings the assembly to a vote first on the motion to commit, and if that motion fails, next on the privileged question. After the privileged question is voted on; the previous question is exhausted, and the consideration of the subject which was interrupted is resumed.

(*c*) Suppose, again that while an amendment to the question is pending a motion is made to refer the subject to a committee, and some one moves to amend this last motion by giving the committee instructions; in

---

many be the easiest way to look at this question, and it makes it as simple as adopting an order closing debate [§ 37 *(d)*], as the latter would have the same privileges, and therefore the same complications as the Previous Question.

* Or thus: "Shall the debate now close and the question [or vote] be taken on the amendment?"

† For other methods of closing debate see §§ 37, 38.

addition to the main question we have here only the motions to amend and to commit, and therefore the previous question, if ordered, applies to them all as one question. The chairman immediately puts the question (1) on the committee's instructions, (2) on the motion to commit, and if this is adopted the subject is referred to the committee and the effect of the previous question is exhausted; but if it fails, next (3) on the amendment, and finally (4) on the main question.

NOTE ON THE PREVIOUS QUESTION.—Much of the confusion heretofore existing in regard to the Previous Question has arisen from the great changes which this motion has undergone. As originally designed, and at present used in the English Parliament, the previous question was not intended to suppress debate, but to suppress the main question, and therefore, in England, it is always moved by the enemies of the measure, who then vote in the negative. It was first used in 1604, and was intended to be applied only to delicate questions; it was put in this form, "Shall the main question be put?" and being negatived, the main question was dismissed for that session. Its form was afterwards changed to this, which is used at present, "Shall the main question be *now* put?" and if negatived the question was dismissed, at first only until after the ensuing debate was over, but now, for that day. The motion for the previous question could be debated; when once put to vote, whether decided affirmatively or negatively, it prevented any discussion of the main question, for, if decided affirmatively, the main question was immediately put, and if decided negatively (that is, that the main question be not now put), it was dismissed for the day.

Our Congress has gradually changed the English Previous Question into an entirely different motion, so that, while in England, the mover of the previous question votes against it, in this country he votes for it. At first the previous question was debatable, and if it was negatived the main question was dismissed for the day, as in England. Congress, in 1805, made it undebatable, and in 1860 caused the consideration of the subject to be resumed if the previous question was negatived, thus completely changing it from the English motion. At first its effect was to cut off all motions except the main question, upon which a vote was immediately taken. This was changed in 1840 so as to bring the House to a vote first upon pending amendments, and then upon the main question. In 1848 its effect was changed again so as to bring the House to a vote upon the motion to commit if it had been made, then upon amendments reported by a committee, if any, then upon pend-

MOTIONS AND ORDER OF PRECEDENCE 47

ing amendments, and finally upon the main question. In 1860 Congress decided that the only effect of the previous question, if the motion to postpone were pending, should be to bring the House to a direct vote on the postponement—thus preventing the previous question from cutting off any pending motion, and completing the change this motion had been gradually undergoing. The previous question is now a simple motion to close debate and proceed to voting as described in the above section.

[To prevent the introduction of any improper or useless subject in an ordinary assembly in this country, the proper course is to "object to its consideration" [§ 15] when it is first introduced, which is very similar to the English previous question.]

21. To Postpone to a Certain Day. This motion takes precedence of a motion to Commit, or Amend, or Indefinitely Postpone, and yields to any Privileged [§ 9] or Incidental [§ 8] Question, and to the motion to Lie on the Table, or for the Previous Question. It can be amended by altering the time, and the Previous Question can be applied to it without affecting any other motions pending. It allows of very limited debate [§ 35], and that must not go into the merits of the subject matter any further than is necessary to enable the assembly to judge the propriety of the postponement.

The *Effect* of this motion is to postpone the entire subject to the time specified until which time it cannot be taken up except by a two-thirds vote [§ 13]. When that time arrives it is entitled to be taken up in preference to everything except Privileged Questions. Where several questions are postponed to different times and are not reached then, they shall be considered in the order of the times to which they were postponed. It is not in order to postpone to a time beyond that session [§ 42] of the assembly, except* to the day of the next session, when it comes up with the unfinished business, and consequently takes precedence of new business [§ 44]. If it is desired to hold an adjourned meeting to consider a special subject, the time to which the assembly shall adjourn [§ 10] should be first fixed before making the motion to postpone the subject to that day.

22. To Commit or Refer [or Recommit, as it is called when the subject has been previously committed]. This motion takes precedence of the motions to Amend or

---
* In Congress a motion cannot be postponed to the next session, but it is customary in ordinary societies.

Indefinitely Postpone, and yields to any Privileged [§ 9] or Incidental [§ 8] Question, and also to the motion to Lie on the Table, or for the Previous Question, or to Postpone to a certain day. It can be amended by altering the committee, or giving it instructions. It is debatable, and opens to debate [§ 35] the merits of the question it is proposed to commit.

The *Form* of this motion is, "to refer the subject to a committee." When different committees are proposed they should be voted on in the following order: (1) committee of the whole [§ 32], (2) a standing committee, and (3) a special (or select) committee. The number of a committee is usually decided without the formality of a motion, as in filling blanks [§ 23]: the chairman asks "Of how many shall the committee consist?" and a question is then put upon each number suggested, beginning with the smallest. The number and kind of the committee need not be decided till after it has been voted to refer the subject to a committee.

If the committee is a select one, and the motion does not include the method of appointing it, and there is no standing rule on the subject, the chairman inquires how the committee shall be appointed, and this is usually decided informally. Sometimes the chair "appoints," in which case he names the members of the committee and no vote is taken upon them; or the committee is "nominated" either by the chair or members of the assembly (no member nominating more than one except by general consent), and then they are all voted upon together, except where more nominations are made than the number of the committee, when they shall be voted upon singly.

Where a committee is one for action (a committee of arrangements for holding a public meeting, for example), it should generally be small, and no one placed upon it who is not favorable to the proposed action; and if any such should be appointed, he should ask to be excused. But when the committee is for deliberation or investigation, it is of the utmost importance that all parties be represented on it, so that in committee the fullest discussion may take place, and thus diminish the chances of unpleasant debates in the assembly.

In ordinary assemblies, by judicious appointment of committees, debates upon delicate and troublesome questions can be mostly confined to the committees,

MOTIONS AND ORDER OF PRECEDENCE

which will contain the representative members of all parties. [See Committees, § 28.]

23. To Amend. This motion takes precedence of nothing but the question which it is proposed to amend, and yields to any Privileged [§ 9], Incidental [§ 8], or Subsidiary [§ 7] Question, except to Indefinitely Postpone. It can be applied to all motions except those in the list at the end of this section, which cannot be amended. It can be amended itself, but this "amendment of an amendment" cannot be amended.

An amendment may be inconsistent with one already adopted, or may directly conflict with the spirit of the original motion, but it must have a direct bearing upon the subject of that motion. *To illustrate:* a motion for a vote of thanks could be amended by striking out "thanks" and inserting "censure;" or one condemning certain customs could be amended by adding other customs.

An amendment may be in any of the following forms: (*a*) to *"add"* or *"insert"* certain words or paragraphs; (*b*) to *"strike out"* *certain words or paragraphs, and if this fails it does not preclude any other amendment than the identical one that has been rejected; (*c*) to *"strike out certain words and insert others,"* which motion is indivisible,† and if lost does not preclude another motion to strike out the same words and insert different ones; (*d*) to *"substitute"* another resolution or paragraph on the same subject for the one pending; (*e*) to *"divide the question"* into two or more questions as the mover specifies, so as to get a separate vote on any particular point or points [see § 4].

If a paragraph is inserted it should be perfected by its friends previous to voting on it, as when once inserted it cannot be struck out or amended except by adding to it. The same is true in regard to words to be inserted in a resolution, as when once inserted they cannot be struck out, except by a motion to strike out the paragraph, or such a portion of it as shall make the question an entirely different one from that of inserting

---

* It was formerly customary to state the question on a motion to strike out, thus: "Shall these words stand as a part of the resolution?" In this country it is now treated the same as any other motion.

† In the case of a motion to "strike out A and insert B," while it is indivisible, in amending it, it is considered as two questions, the amendment to the first part, the part to be stricken out, having the precedence. [U.S. Senate Rule 18.]

the particular words. The principle involved is, that when the assembly has voted that certain words shall form a part of a resolution, it is not in order to make another motion which involves exactly the same question as the one it has decided. The only way to bring it up again is to move a Reconsideration [§ 27] of the vote by which the words were inserted.

*Filling Blanks** are usually treated somewhat differently from other amendments, in that any number of members may propose, without a second, different numbers for filling the blank, and these are treated not as amendments of one another, but as independent propositions to be voted on successively, the smallest sum and longest time being put first.

Nominations are treated in a similar manner, so that a second nomination is not regarded as an amendment of the first, but as an independent motion to be voted on if the first fails to receive a majority vote. Any number of nominations can be made, the chairman announcing each name as he hears it, and they should be voted for in the order announced until one receives a vote sufficient for election, which is a majority unless the By-Laws prescribe a different number.

The numbers prefixed to paragraphs are only marginal indications, and should be corrected, if necessary, by the clerk, without any motion to amend.

An Amendment to Rules of Order, By-Laws or a Constitution shall require previous notice and a two-thirds vote for his adoption [see § 45].

[For amending reports of Committees and propositions containing several paragraphs, see § 31; for amending minutes, see § 41; for the proper form of stating the question on an amendment, see § 65.]

The following motions *cannot be amended:*

To Adjourn (when unqualified)	See § 11
For the Orders of the Day	" § 13
All Incidental Questions	" § 8
To Lay on the Table	" § 19
For the Previous Question	" § 20
An Amendment of an Amendment	" § 23
To Postpone Indefinitely	" § 24
To Reconsider	" § 27

---

* In the U.S. House of Representatives filling blanks are treated as other amendments The practice of the Senate, as that of the English Parliament, is given above. The Senate, until the last revision of its rules, gives precedence to the largest instead of the smallest sum.

Note on Amendments.—A resolution is amended by altering the words of the resolution; an amendment is amended by altering the words of the amendment, that is, by altering the words to be inserted or to be stricken out. The form of the motion cannot be amended; that is, a motion to adopt a resolution cannot be amended so as to substitute a motion to reject the resolution, as this alters the form, not the words of the resolution; a motion to "strike out A" cannot be amended by adding "and insert B," so as to read, "strike out A and insert B," which is another form of amendment, and is not an alteration of "A"; a motion to "insert B before the word C" in a resolution, cannot be amended by substituting another resolution for the one pending, thus changing the form of the amendment and not simply altering "B"; a motion to "insert B before the word C" cannot be amended by adding "and D before the word E," because the only thing that can be altered in the pending amendment is "B," the other words being those that are necessary to describe what it is proposed to do with "B."

If the pending amendment is to "insert A B C D before F," it is in order to apply any form of amendment to "A B C D," and no amendment is in order that is not confined to simply altering those words, "A B C D."

When a member desires to move an amendment that is not in order at the time but affects the pending question, he should state his intention of offering his amendment if the pending amendment is voted down. In this way those who favor his amendment will vote in the negative, and if they succeed in killing it, then the new amendment can be offered.

24. To Postpone Indefinitely. This motion takes precedence of nothing except the Principal Question [§ 6], and yields to any Privileged [§ 9], Incidental [§ 8], or Subsidiary [§ 7] Motion, except to Amend. It can be applied to nothing but a Principal Question [§ 6] and a Question of Privilege [§ 12]. It cannot be amended; it opens to debate the entire question which it is proposed to postpone. Its effect* is to entirely remove the question from before the assembly for that session [§ 42]. The Previous Question [§ 20], if ordered when this motion is pending, applies only to it without affecting the main question.

---

* An affirmative vote on this question is identical in effect with a negative vote on the main question. Its only value is when the opposition is doubtful of its strength, because if defeated on this motion they still have an opportunity for further struggle for victory, which would not be the case if they had been defeated on a vote on the main question.

Miscellaneous Motions.
[§§ 25-27.]

25. Rescind. When an assembly wishes to annul some action it has previously taken and it is too late to reconsider [§ 27] the vote, the proper course to pursue is to Rescind the objectionable resolution, order, or other proceeding. This motion has no privilege but stands on a footing with a new resolution. Any action of the body can be rescinded regardless of the time that has elapsed.*

26. Renewal of a Motion. When any Principal Question [§ 6] or Amendment has been once acted upon by the assembly, it cannot be taken up again at the same session [§ 42] except by a motion to Reconsider [§ 27], and when the motion to reconsider has been once acted upon, it, the motion to reconsider, cannot be repeated on the same question unless the question was amended when previously reconsidered. A correction of the minutes [§ 41], however, can be made without a motion to reconsider, at the same or any subsequent session, and so can a motion to rescind [§ 25]. The motion to Adjourn [§ 11] can be renewed if there has been progress in debate, or any business transacted. As a general rule the introduction of any motion that alters the state of affairs makes it admissible to renew any Privileged or Incidental Motion (excepting a motion for the Orders of the Day or for the Suspension of the Rules as provided in §§ 13, 18), or Subsidiary Motion (excepting an Amendment), as in such a case the real question before the assembly is a different one.

To illustrate: a motion that a question lie on the table having failed, suppose afterwards it be moved to refer the matter to a committee, it is now in order to move again that the subject lie on the table: but such a motion would not be in order if it were not made till after the failure of the motion to commit, as the question then resumes its previous condition. So, if a subject has been taken from the table or an objection to its consideration has been voted down, it is not in order

---

* Where it is desired not only to rescind the action but to express very strong disapproval, legislative bodies have on rare occasions voted to rescind the objectionable resolution and expunge it from the record, which is done by crossing out the words, or drawing a line around them, and writing across them the words "Expunged by order of the assembly, etc.," giving the date of the order.

to move to lay it on the table, as this practically involves the very question the assembly has just decided.

When a subject has been referred to a committee which reports at the same meeting, the matter stands before the assembly as if it had been introduced for the first time. A motion which has been withdrawn has not been acted upon, and therefore can be renewed.

27. Reconsider. It is in order at any time, even when another member has the floor, or while the assembly is voting on the motion to Adjourn, during the day on which a motion has been acted upon, or the next succeeding day,* to move to "Reconsider the vote" and have such motion "entered on the record," but it cannot be considered while another question is before the assembly It must be made, excepting when the vote is by ballot, by a member who voted with the prevailing side;† for instance, in case a motion fails to pass for lack of a two-thirds vote, a reconsideration must be moved by one who voted against the motion.

A motion to reconsider the vote on a Subsidiary [§ 7] Motion takes precedence of the main question. It yields to Privileged [§ 9] Questions (except for the Orders of the Day) and Incidental [§ 8] Questions.

This motion can be *applied*‡ to the vote on every other question, except to Adjourn and to Suspend the Rules, and an affirmative vote on to Lay on the Table or to Take from the Table [§ 19], and a vote electing to office one who is present and does not decline. No question can be twice reconsidered,** unless it was amended after its first reconsideration. If an amendment to a motion has been either adopted or rejected, and then a vote taken on the motion as amended, it is not in order to reconsider the vote on the amendment until after the vote on the original motion has been reconsidered.

---

* If the vote is not reconsidered on the day it was taken, and no meeting is held the next day, then it cannot be reconsidered at the next meeting. The proper course then is to renew the motion if it failed, or rescind [§ 25] it if it had been adopted.

† Any one can second the motion. In Congress any one can move a reconsideration, excepting where the vote is taken by yeas and nays [§ 38], when the rule above applies.

‡ It is not the practice to reconsider an affirmative vote on the motion to lay on the table, as the same results can be reached by the motion to take from the table. For a similar reason, an affirmative vote on a motion to take from the table cannot be reconsidered.

** The minutes can be corrected any number of times without a reconsideration.

If the Previous Question [§ 20] has been partly executed, it cannot be reconsidered. If anything which the assembly cannot reverse has been done as the result of a vote, then that vote cannot be reconsidered. This motion cannot be amended; it is debatable or not, just as the question to be reconsidered is debatable or undebatable [§ 35]; when debatable, it opens up for discussion the entire subject to be reconsidered, and the Previous Question [§ 20], if ordered while it is pending, affects only the motion to reconsider. It can be laid on the table [§ 19], in which case, the reconsideration, like any other question, can be taken from the table, but possesses no privilege.* The motion to reconsider being laid on the table does not carry with it the pending measure.

The *Effect of making* this motion is to suspend all action that the original motion would have required until the reconsideration is acted upon; but if it is not called up, its effect terminates with the session [§ 42], provided,† that in an assembly having regular meetings as often as monthly, if there is not held upon another day an adjourned meeting of the one at which the reconsideration was moved, its effect shall not terminate till the close of the next succeeding session [see note at end of this section]. But the reconsideration of an Incidental [§ 8] or Subsidiary [§ 7] Motion (except where the vote to be reconsidered had the effect to remove the whole subject from before the assembly) shall be immediately acted upon, as otherwise it would prevent action on the main question.‡

---

* In Congress it is usual for the member in charge of an important bill as soon as it passes to move its reconsideration, and at the same time to move that the motion to reconsider be laid on the table. If the latter motion is adopted it is deemed a finality, as the number of bills on the calendar precludes its ever being taken up except by a two-thirds vote. But this is not so in an ordinary society. There is no good reason in this case for violating the general principle that only one motion can be made at a time.

† In Congress the effect always terminates with the session, and it cannot be called up by any one but the mover, until the expiration of the time during which it is in order to move a reconsideration.

‡ Thus, suppose the motion to Indefinitely Postpone is negatived, showing that the assembly wish to consider the subject ; if it is moved to reconsider the last vote, then the reconsideration must be immediately acted upon, as otherwise the whole subject would be removed from before the assembly as shown above, without any possible benefit to the assembly If the object is to prevent a temporary majority from adopting a resolution, the proper course is to wait until the resolution is finally acted upon, and then move the reconsideration. If the motion to Indefinitely

MOTIONS AND ORDER OF PRECEDENCE 55

While this motion is so highly privileged as far as relates to having it entered on the minutes, yet the reconsideration of another question cannot be made to interfere with the discussion of a question before the assembly, but as soon as that subject is disposed of, the reconsideration, if called up,* takes precedence of everything except the motions to adjourn, and to fix the time to which to adjourn. As long as its effect lasts (as shown above), any one can call up the motion to reconsider, and have it acted upon—excepting that when its effect extends beyond the meeting at which the motion was made, no one but the mover can call it up at that meeting.

The *Effect of the adoption* of this motion is to place before the assembly the original question in the exact position it occupied before it was voted upon; consequently no one can debate the question reconsidered who had previously exhausted his right to debate [§ 34] on that question; his only resource is to discuss the question while the motion to reconsider is before the assembly. When a vote taken under the operation of the previous question is reconsidered, the question is then divested of the previous question, and is open to debate and amendment, provided the previous question had been exhausted [see § 20] by votes taken on all the questions covered by it, before the motion to reconsider was made.

A reconsideration requires only a majority vote, regardless of the vote necessary to adopt the motion reconsidered [For reconsidering in committee see § 28.]

NOTE ON RECONSIDER.—In the English Parliament a vote once taken cannot be reconsidered, but in our Congress it is allowed to move a reconsideration of the vote on the same or succeeding day, and after the close of the last day for making the motion, anyone can call up the motion to reconsider, so that this motion cannot delay action more than two days, and the effect of the motion, if not acted upon, terminates with the session. There seems to be no reason or good precedent for permitting merely two persons, by moving a reconsideration, to suspend for any length of time all action under resolutions adopted by the as-

---

Postpone is carried, the subject is removed from before the assembly, and consequently there is no hinderance to business in permitting the reconsideration to hold over to another day.

* When the reconsideration has been called up it can be treated as other motions, and holds over as unfinished business.

sembly, and yet where the delay is very short the advantages of reconsideration overbalance the evil.

Where a permanent society has meetings weekly or monthly, and usually only a small proportion of the society is present, it seems best to allow a reconsideration to hold over to another meeting, so that the society may have notice of what action is about to be taken. To prevent the motion being used to defeat a measure that cannot be deferred till the next regular meeting, it is provided that in case the society adjourns, to meet on a different day, then the reconsideration will not hold over beyond that session; this allows sufficient delay to notify the society, while, if the question is one requiring immediate action, the delay cannot extend beyond the day to which it adjourns. The rule provides that the adjourned meeting must be held on another day, in order to prevent the whole object of the reconsideration being defeated by an immediate adjournment to meet again in a few minutes. Where the meetings are only quarterly or annual the society should be properly represented at each meeting, and their best interests are subserved by following the practice of Congress, and letting the effect of the reconsideration terminate with the session.

Art. IV. Committees and Informal Action
[§§ 28-33.]

28. **Committees.**[*] It is usual in deliberative assemblies, to have all preliminary work in the preparation of matter for their action done by means of committees. These may be either "standing committees" (which are appointed for the session [§ 42], or for some definite time, as one year); or "select committees," appointed for a special purpose; or a "committee of the whole" [§ 32], consisting of the entire assembly. [For method of appointing committees of the whole, see § 32; other committees, see Commit, § 22.] The first person named on a committee is chairman (in his absence the next

---

[*] An ex-officio member of a committee or Board is one who is a member by virtue of holding some particular office. If the office is under the control of the Society, then there is no distinction between the ex-officio member and the other members. But if the ex-officio member is not under the authority of the Society, he has all the privileges but none of the obligations of membership, as where the Governor of a State is ex-officio a manager or a trustee of a private academy. Sometimes the By-laws provide that the President shall be ex-officio a member of every committee; in such a case it is evidently the intention to permit, not to require, him to act as a member of the various committees, and therefore in counting a quorum he should not be counted as a member. The President is not a member of any committee except by virtue of a special rule, unless he is so appointed by the assembly.

named member becomes chairman, and so on), and should act as such, unless the committee, by a majority of its number, elects another chairman, which it is competent to do, unless the assembly has appointed the chairman. The clerk should furnish him, or some other member of the committee, with notice of the appointment of the committee, giving the names of the members, the matter referred to them, and such instructions as the assembly have decided upon. The chairman shall call the committee together, and, if there is a quorum (a majority of the committee, see § 43), he should read, or have read, the entire resolutions referred to them; he should then read each paragraph, and pause for amendments to be offered; when the amendments to that paragraph are voted on he proceeds to the next, only taking votes on amendments, as the committee cannot vote on the adoption of matter referred to them by the assembly.

If the committee originate the resolutions, they vote, in the same way, on amendments to each paragraph of the draft of the resolutions (which draft has been previously prepared by one of their members or a subcommittee); they do not vote on the separate paragraphs, but, having completed the amendments, they vote on the adoption of the entire report [see § 31]. When there is a preamble it is considered last. If the report originates with the committee, all amendments are to be incorporated in the report; but if the resolutions were referred, the committee cannot alter the text, but must submit the original paper intact, with their amendments (which may be in the form of a substitute, § 23) written on a separate sheet.

A committee is a miniature assembly that must meet together in order to transact business, and usually one of its members should be appointed its clerk. Whatever is not agreed to by the majority of the members present at a meeting (at which a quorum, consisting of a majority of the members of the committee, shall be present) cannot form a part of its report. The minority may be permitted to submit their views in writing also, either together, or each member separately, but their reports can only be acted upon by voting to substitute one of them for the report of the committee [see § 30]. The rules of the assembly, as far as possible, shall apply in committee;* but a reconsideration [§ 27] of a vote shall be allowed, regardless of the time elapsed, only when every member who voted with the majority is present when the reconsideration is moved.† A committee (except a committee of the whole, § 32) may appoint a sub-committee. When through with the business assigned them, a motion is made for the committee to "rise" (which is equivalent to the motion to adjourn), and that the chairman (or some member who is more familiar with the subject) make its report to the assembly. The committee ceases to exist as soon as the assembly receives the report [§ 30], unless it is a standing committee.

The committee has no power to punish its members for disorderly conduct, its resource being to report the facts to the assembly. No allusion can be made in the assembly to what has occurred in committee, except it be by a report of the committee, or by general consent. It is the duty of a committee to meet on the call of any two of its members, if the chairman is absent or declines to appoint such meeting. When a committee adjourns without appointing a time for the next meeting, it is called together in the same way as at its first meeting. When a committee adjourns to meet at another time, it is not necessary (though usually advisable) that absent members should be notified of the adjourned meeting.

29. Forms of Reports of Committees.

The form of a report is usually similar to the following:

A standing committee reports thus: "The committee on [insert name of committee] respectfully report" [or "beg leave to report, or "beg leave to submit the following report"], etc., letting the report follow.

A select or special committee reports as follows: "The committee to which was referred [state the matter re-

---

* The chairman of a committee usually takes the most active part in the discussion and work of the committee. A second is not required to a motion, nor, except in large committees, is one required to stand while speaking. In small committees motions may be dispensed with, but a vote should always be taken so as to know exactly what has been decided.

† Both the English common parliamentary law and the rules of Congress prohibit the reconsideration of a vote by a committee, but the strict enforcement of this rule in ordinary committees would interfere with rather than assist the transaction of business. The rule given above seems more just, and more in accordance with the practice of ordinary committees, who usually reconsider at pleasure. No improper advantage can be taken of the privilege, as long as every member who voted with the majority must be present when the reconsideration is moved.

ferred] having considered the same, respectfully report," etc. Or for "The committee" is sometimes written "Your committee," or "The undersigned, a committee."

When a minority report is submitted, it should be in this form, the majority reporting as above: "The undersigned, a minority of a committee to which we referred," etc. The majority report is the report of the committee, and should never be made out as the report of the majority.

Reports sometimes conclude with, "All of which is respectfully submitted," but this is not necessary. They are sometimes signed only by the chairman of the committee, but if the matter is of much importance, it is better that the report be signed by every member who concurs. The report is not usually dated or addressed, but can be headed, as, for example, "Report of the Finance Committee of the Y. P. A., on Renting a Hall." The report of a committee should generally close or be accompanied with formal resolutions covering all its recommendations, so that the adopting of their report [§ 31] would have the effect to adopt all the resolutions necessary to carry out their recommendations.* The committee may be able to perform the entire duty assigned it by reporting a resolution, in which case the resolution alone is submitted in writing.

30. Reception of Reports. When the report of a committee is to be made, the chairman (or member appointed to make the report) informs the assembly that the committee to whom was referred such a subject or paper, has directed him to make a report thereon, or report it with or without amendment, as the case may be; either he or any other member may move that it be "received"† now or at some other specified time.

Usually the formality of a vote on the reception of a report of a committee is dispensed with, the time being settled by general consent. Should any one object, a

---

* If the report of a committee were written in this form, "Your committee think the conduct of Mr. A. at the last meeting so disgraceful that they would recommend that he be expelled from the society," the adoption of the report would not have the effect to expel the member.

† A very common error is, after a report has been read, to move that it be received; whereas the fact that it has been read shows that it has been already received by the assembly. Another mistake, less common, but dangerous, is to vote that the report be accepted (which is equivalent to adopting it, see § 31), when the intention is only to have the report up for consideration and afterwards move its adoption. Still a third error is, to

formal motion becomes necessary. When the time arrives for the assembly to receive the report, the chairman of the committee reads it in his place* and then delivers it to the clerk, when it lies on the table till the assembly sees fit to consider it. If the report consists of a paper with amendments, the chairman of the committee reads the amendments with the coherence in the paper, explaining the alterations and the reasons of the committee for the amendments, till he has gone through the whole. If the report is very long it is not usually read until the assembly is ready to consider it [see § 31].

When the report has been received, whether it has been read or not, the committee is thereby dissolved, and can act no more unless it is revived by a vote to recommit. If the report is recommitted, all the parts of the report that have not been agreed to by the assembly are ignored by the committee as if the report had never been made.

If any member or members wish to submit a minority report (or reports) it is customary to receive it immediately after receiving the report of the committee; but it cannot be acted upon unless a motion is made to substitute it for the report of the committee.

31. Adoption of Reports.† When the assembly is to consider a report, if it has not been already done, a motion should be made to "adopt," "accept," or "agree to" the report, all of which, when carried, have the same effect, namely, to make the doings of the committee become the acts of the assembly, the same as if done by the assembly without the intervention of a committee, and therefore if the report contains formal resolutions it adopts those resolutions. While these motions are generally used indiscriminately, and all have the same effect, still it would probably be better to vary the

---

move that "the report be adopted and the committee be discharged," when the committee has reported in full and its report has been received, so that the committee has already ceased to exist. If the committee, however, has made but a partial report, or report progress, then it is in order to move that the committee be discharged from the further consideration of the subject.

---

* As soon as he has read the report it is well for him to move its acceptance [or adoption], or whatever motion is necessary to carry out the committee's recommendations.

† When the committee's report is only for the information of the assembly, it is not necessary to take any action on it after it has been read.

COMMITTEES AND INFORMAL ACTION

motion according to the character of the report. Thus, if the report contains merely a statement of opinion or facts, the best form of the motion is to "accept the report;" if it also concludes with resolutions or orders, the motion would be more appropriately "to agree to the resolutions," or "to adopt the orders."* If either of these latter motions is carried, the effect is to adopt the entire report of the committee.

After either of the above motions is made, the report is open to amendment,† and the matter stands before the assembly exactly the same as if there had been no committee, and the subject had been introduced by the motion of the member who made the report.

When a committee reports back a resolution which was referred to it, the question should be stated as follow: (a) If the committee recommends its adoption, or makes no recommendation, or recommends that it be not adopted, in either case the question should be on adopting the resolution. In the latter case it might be well to adopt a form similar to this: "The question is on the adoption of the resolution, the report of the committee to the contrary notwithstanding." (b) If the committee recommends that the resolution be indefinitely postponed, or postponed to a certain time, the question should be on the indefinite postponement, or the postponement to the certain time. (c) If the committee recommends that the resolution be amended in a certain way, then the question should be on the adoption of the proposed amendment to the resolution, and then on adopting the resolution. In all these cases, immediately after the committee's report is read, some one should make the proper motion indicated above, and the proper person to make it, if the committee makes any recommendation, is the member of the committee who makes the report. If no motion is made, the

---

* "To adopt" the report is the most common of these motions in ordinary societies, and is used regardless of the character of the report. Its effect is generally understood, which is not the case with the motion to accept, as shown in the note to § 30 [which see for common errors in acting upon reports]. The last paragraph of § 29 shows how the form of the report influences the effect of its adoption.

† In the case of an annual report of an Executive Committee or Board of Managers which is published as their report, care should be taken in amending it to show clearly for what the Board is responsible and for what the Society. This can be done by prefixing to the report the statement that "The Report was adopted by the Society after striking out what is inclosed in brackets and adding what is printed in footnotes."

chairman may ask if some one will not make such and such a motion, stating the proper one, or he may state the question without further delay, assuming the proper motion to have been made. [See § 65, 1st note.]

When a committee submits a report containing a number of paragraphs or sections, as for instance a set of By-Laws, the whole paper should be read through by either the member reporting it, or the clerk, and the member reporting it, or some one else, should move its adoption, unless this has been previously done. The chairman having stated the question on the adoption of the report, he should direct the member who reported it, or the clerk, to read the first paragraph,* and when it has been read, inquire, "Are there any amendments proposed to this paragraph?" He should then pause for any remarks or amendments, always giving the preference to the member who submitted the report if he wishes the floor. When satisfied no one else desires the floor, he should say, "No amendments (or no further amendments) being offered to this paragraph, the next will be read." In this way each paragraph is read and amended, when the chair states that the entire report, or all of the resolutions, have been read and are open to amendment. At this stage new paragraphs may be inserted, or even those originally in the report may be further amended, as they have not yet been adopted. If there is a preamble it should be read and amended after the body of the resolutions has been perfected, and then a vote is taken on adopting the entire report as amended.

When a committee reports back a paper with amendments, the reporting member reads only the amendments and then moves their adoption. The chairman, after stating the question on the adoption of the amend-

---

* By "paragraphs" is meant in this rule the separate divisions of the proposition, and they may be Articles, Sections, Paragraphs, or separate resolutions.

No vote should be taken on the adoption of the several paragraphs, one vote being taken finally on the adoption of the whole paper. By not adopting separately the different paragraphs, it is in order, after they have all been amended, to go back and amend any of them still further. In committee a similar paper would be treated the same way [see § 28]. In § 48 (b) an illustration is given of the practical application of this section.

If each paragraph or section is adopted separately, it is improper afterwards to vote on the adoption of the whole report, as this would be voting to adopt what has been already adopted in detail. So, too, it is out of order to go back and amend a paragraph that has been adopted, until after it has been reconsidered.

ments, calls for the reading of the first amendment, after which it is open for debate and amendment. A vote is then taken on adopting this amendment, and the next is read, and so on till the amendments are adopted or rejected, admitting amendments to the committee's amendments, but no others. When through with the committee's amendments, the chairman pauses for any other amendments to be proposed by the assembly; and when these are voted on he puts the question on agreeing to, or adopting, the paper as amended, unless in a case like revising the By-Laws, where they have been already adopted. By "suspending the rules" [§ 18], or by general consent, a report can be at once adopted without following any of the above routine. [See § 34 for the privileges in debate of the member making the report.]

32. **Committee of the Whole.** When an assembly has to consider a subject which it does not wish to refer to a committee, and yet where the subject matter is not well digested and put into proper form for its definite action, or when, for any other reason, it is desirable for the assembly to consider a subject with all the freedom of an ordinary committee, it is the practice to refer the matter to the "Committee of the Whole."* If it is desired to consider the question at once, the motion is made, "That the assembly do now resolve itself into a committee of the whole, to take under consideration," etc., specifying the subject. This is really a motion to "commit." [See § 22 for its order of precedence, etc.] If adopted, the chairman immediately calls another member to the chair, and takes his place as a member of the committee. The committee is under the rules of the assembly, excepting as stated hereafter in this section.

The only motions in order are to amend and adopt, and that the committee "rise and report," as it cannot adjourn; nor can it order the "yeas and nays" [§ 38]. The only way to close or limit debate in committee of the whole is for the assembly to vote that the debate in committee shall cease at a certain time, or that after a

---

* In large assemblies, such as the U.S. House of Representatives, where a member can speak to any question but once, the committee of the whole seems almost a necessity, as it allows the freest discussion of a subject, while at any time it can rise and thus bring into force the strict rules of the assembly.

certain time no debate shall be allowed, excepting on new amendments, and then only one speech in favor of and one against it, of say five minutes each; or in some other way regulate the time for debate.*

If no limit is prescribed, any member may speak as often as he can get the floor, and as long each time as is allowed in debate in the assembly, provided no one wishes the floor who has not spoken on that particular question. Debate having been closed at a particular time by order of the assembly, it is not competent for the committee, even by unanimous consent, to extend the time. The committee cannot refer the subject to another committee. Like other committees [§ 28], it cannot alter the text of any resolution referred to it; but if the resolution originated in the committee, then all the amendments are incorporated in it.

When it is through with the consideration of the subject referred to it, or if it wishes to adjourn, or to have the assembly limit debate, a motion is made that "the committee rise and report," etc., specifying the result of its proceedings. This motion "to rise" is equivalent to the motion to adjourn in the assembly, and is always in order (except when another member has the floor), and is undebatable. As soon as this motion is adopted the presiding officer takes the chair, and the chairman of the committee, having resumed his place in the assembly, rises and informs him that "the committee has gone through the business referred to it, and that he is ready to make the report when the assembly is ready to receive it;" or he will make such other report as will suit the case.

The clerk does not record the proceedings of the committee on the minutes, but should keep a memorandum of the proceedings for the use of the committee. In large assemblies the clerk vacates his chair, which is occupied by the chairman of the committee, and the assistant clerk acts as clerk of the committee. Should the committee get disorderly, and the chairman be unable

* In Congress no motion to limit debate in committee of the whole is in order till after the subject has been already considered in committee of the whole. As no subject would probably be considered more than once in committee of the whole, in an ordinary society, the enforcement of this rule would practically prevent such a society from putting any limit to debate in the committee. The rule, as given above, allows the society, whenever resolving itself into committee of the whole, to impose upon the debate in the committee such restrictions as are allowed in Congress after the subject has already been considered in committee of the whole.

to preserve order, the presiding officer can take the chair, and declare the committee dissolved. The quorum of the committee of the whole is the same as that of the assembly [§ 43]. If the committee finds itself without a quorum, it can only rise and report the fact to the assembly, which in such a case would have to adjourn.

33. Informal Consideration of a Question (or acting *as if in committee of the whole*).

It has become customary in many assemblies, instead of going into committee of the whole, to consider the question "informally" and afterwards to act "formally." In a small assembly there is no objection to this.* While acting informally upon any resolutions, the assembly can only amend and adopt them, and without further motion the chairman announces that "the assembly, acting informally [or as in committee of the whole], has had such subject under consideration, and has made certain amendments, which he will report." The subject comes before the assembly then as if reported by a committee. While acting informally the chairman retains his seat, as it is not necessary to move that the committee rise; but at any time the adoption of such motions as to adjourn, the previous question, to commit, or any motion except to amend or adopt, puts an end to the informal consideration; as, for example, the motion to commit is equivalent to the following motions when in committee of the whole: (1) That the committee rise; (2) that the committee of the whole be discharged from the further consideration of the subject; and (3) that it be referred to a committee.

While acting informally, every member can speak as many times as he pleases, and as long each time as permitted in the assembly [§ 34], and the informal action may be rejected or altered by the assembly. While the clerk should keep a memorandum of the informal proceedings, it should not be entered on the minutes, being only for temporary use. The chairman's report to the assembly of the informal action should be entered on the minutes, as it belongs to the assembly's proceedings.

---

* In the U.S. Senate all bills, joint resolutions and treaties, upon their second reading are considered "as if the Senate were in committee of the whole," which is equivalent to considering them informally. [U.S. Senate Rules, 28 and 38.] In large assemblies it is better to follow the practice of the House of Representatives, and go into committee of the whole.

Art. V. Debate and Decorum
[§§ 34-37.]

34. Debate.* When a motion is made and seconded, it shall be stated by the chairman before being debated [see § 3]. When any member is about to speak in debate he shall rise and respectfully address himself to "Mr. Chairman." ["Mr. President" is used where that is the designated title of the presiding officer; "Mr. Moderator"† is more common in religious meetings. In every case the presiding officer should be addressed by his official title.] The chairman shall then announce his name. By parliamentary courtesy,‡ the member upon whose motion a subject is brought before the assembly is first entitled to the floor [see § 2], even though another member has risen first and addressed the chair [in case of a report of a committee it is the member who presents the report]; and he is also entitled to close the debate, but not until every member choosing to speak has spoken. When a member reports a measure from a committee, he cannot in any way be deprived of his right to close the debate; so if the previous question [§20] is ordered the chairman at once assigns him the floor to close the debate. With this exception, no member shall speak more than twice to the same question (only once to a question of order § 14), nor longer than ten minutes at one time, without leave of the assembly, and the question upon granting the leave shall be decided by a two-thirds vote [§ 39] without debate.** If greater freedom is desired, the proper course is to refer the subject to the committee of the whole [§ 32], or to consider it informally [§ 33]. [For limiting or closing the debate see § 37.]

No member can speak the second time to a question until every member choosing to speak has spoken. But an amendment, or any other motion, being offered,

---

* In connection with this section read §§ 1-5.

† "Brother Moderator" is more commonly used in some sections of the country; but in strictness of speech it implies an official equality between the speaker and the chairman that does not exist, or in other words it implies that they are both moderators. If a woman is in the chair, the only change in the address is by substituting "Mrs." or "Miss," as the case may be, for "Mr." Thus, "Madam," for "Mr." Thus, "Mrs. President."

‡ The U.S. House of Representatives provides for this by rule.

** The limit in time should vary to suit circumstances, but the limit of two speeches of ten minutes each will usually answer in ordinary assemblies, and when desirable, by a two-thirds vote it can be increased, as

DEBATE AND DECORUM

makes the real question before the assembly a different one, and, in regard to the right to debate, is treated as a new question. Merely asking a question, or making a suggestion, is not considered as speaking. The maker of a motion, though he can vote against it, cannot speak against his own motion.

When an amendment is pending the debate must be confined to the merits of the amendment, unless it is of such a nature that its decision practically decides the main question.

The chairman cannot close the debate as long as any member desires to speak, and should a member claim the floor after the chairman has risen to put the question, or even after the affirmative vote has been taken, provided the negative has not been put, he has a right to resume the debate or make a motion.

35. Undebatable Questions and those Opening the Main Question to Debate. The following questions shall be decided without debate, all others being debatable [see note at end of this section]:

To *Fix the Time to which the Assembly shall Adjourn* (when a privileged question, § 10).

To *Adjourn* [§ 11], (or in committee, *to rise*, which is used instead of to adjourn).

For the *Orders of the Day* [§ 13], and questions relating to the *priority of business*.

An *Appeal* [§ 14], when made while the Previous Question is pending, or when simply relating to indecorum or transgressions of the rules of speaking, or to the priority of business.

Objection to the Consideration of a Question [§ 15].

To *Lay on the Table*, or to *Take from the Table* [§ 19].

The *Previous Question* [§ 20].

To *Reconsider* [§ 27] a question which is itself undebatable,

Questions relating to *Reading of Papers* [§ 16], or *Withdrawing a Motion* [§ 17], or *Suspending the Rules* [§ 18] or *extending the limits of debate* [§ 34], or *limit-*

---

shown above, or diminished as shown in § 37. In the U.S. House of Representatives no member can speak more than once to the same question, nor longer than one hour. The fourth rule of the Senate is as follows: "No senator shall speak more than twice in any one debate, on the same day, without leave of the Senate, which question shall be decided without debate." If no rule is adopted, each member can speak but once to the same question.

ing or closing debate [§ 37], or granting *leave to continue his* speech to one who has been guilty of indecorum in debate [§ 36].

The motion *to postpone to a certain time*, [§ 21] allows of but very limited debate, which must be confined to the propriety of the postponement. When an *amendment* is before the assembly the main question cannot be debated excepting so far as it is necessarily involved in the amendment. But the following motions open to discussion the entire merits of the main question:

To Commit [§ 22].
To Postpone Indefinitely [§ 24].
To Rescind [§ 25].
To Reconsider a debatable question [§ 27].

The distinction between debate and making suggestions or asking a question should always be kept in view, and, when the latter will assist the assembly in determining the question, is allowed, to a limited extent, even though the question before the assembly is undebatable.

Note on Undebatable Questions.—The English common parliamentary law makes all motions debatable, unless there is a rule adopted limiting debate; but every assembly is obliged to restrict debate upon certain motions. The restrictions to debate prescribed in this section conform to the practice of Congress, where, however, it is very common to allow of brief remarks upon the most undebatable questions, sometimes five or six members speaking. This, of course, is allowed only when no one objects.

By examining the above list it will be found that, while free debate is allowed upon every principal question [§ 6], it is permitted or prohibited upon other questions in accordance with the following principles:

(a) Highly privileged questions, as a rule, should not be debated, as in that case they could be used to prevent the assembly from coming to a vote on the main question (for instance, if the motion to adjourn were debatable, it could be used [see § 11] in a way to greatly hinder business). *High privilege is, as a rule, incompatible with the right of debate on the privileged question.*

(b) A motion that has the effect to suppress a question before the assembly, so that it cannot again be taken up that session [§ 42], allows of free debate; and a Subsidiary Motion [§ 7, except Commit, which see below], is debatable to just the extent that it interferes with the right of the assembly to take up the original question at its pleasure.

Illustrations: To "Indefinitely Postpone" [§ 24] a question places it out of the power of the assembly to again take it up during that session, and consequently this motion allows of free debate, even involving the whole merits of the original question.

To "Postpone to a certain time" prevents the assembly taking up the question till the specified time, and therefore allows of limited debate upon the propriety of the postponement.

To "Lay on the Table" leaves the question so that the assembly can at any time consider it, and therefore should not be, and is not debatable.*

To "Commit" would not be very debatable, according to this rule, but it is an exception, because it is often important that the committee should know the views of the assembly on the question, and it therefore is not only debatable, but opens to debate the whole question which it is proposed to refer to the committee.

36. Decorum in Debate [see § 2]. In debate a member must confine himself to the question before the assembly, and avoid personalities. He cannot reflect upon any act of the assembly, unless he intends to conclude his remarks with a motion to rescind such action or else while debating such motion. In referring to another member, he should, as much as possible, avoid using his name, rather referring to him as "the member who spoke last," or in some other way describing him. The officers of the assembly should always be referred to by their official titles. It is not allowable to arraign the motives of a member, but the nature or consequences of a measure may be condemned in strong terms. It is not the man, but the measure, that is the subject of debate. If at any time the chairman rises to state a point of order, or give information, or otherwise speak, within his privilege [see § 40], the member speaking must take his seat till the chairman has been first heard. When called to order, the member must sit down until the question of order is decided. If his remarks are decided to be improper, he cannot proceed, if any one objects, without the leave of the assembly expressed by a vote, upon which question there shall be no debate.

Disorderly words should be taken down by the member who objects to them, or by the clerk, and then read to the member; if he denies them, the assembly shall decide by a vote whether they are his words or not. If a member cannot justify the words he used, and will not

---

* See Note at close of § 19 for abuses of this motion.

suitably apologize for using them, it is the duty of the assembly to act in the case. If the disorderly words are of a personal nature, before the assembly proceeds to deliberate upon the case both parties to the personality should retire, it being a general rule that no member should be present in the assembly when any matter relating to himself is under debate. It is not, however, necessary for the member objecting to the words to retire unless he is personally involved in the case. If any business has taken place since the member spoke, it is too late to take notice of any disorderly words he used.

During debate, and while the chairman is speaking, or the assembly is engaged in voting, no member is permitted to disturb the assembly by whispering, or walking across the floor, or in any other way.

37. Closing Debate. Debate upon a question is not closed by the chairman rising to put the question, as, until both the affirmative and negative are put, a member can claim the floor, and reopen debate [see § 38]. Debate can be closed by the following motions,* which are undebatable [§ 35], and, except to Lay on the Table, shall require a two-thirds† vote for their adoption [§ 39]:

(a) *An Objection to the Consideration of a Question* [§ 15], which is allowable only when the question is first introduced, and if sustained, not only stops debate, but also throws the subject out of the assembly for that session [§ 42]; which latter effect is the one for which it was designed.

(b) To *Lay on the Table* [§ 19], which, if adopted, carries the question to the table, from which it cannot be taken unless a majority favor such action.

(c) The *Previous Question* [§ 20], which, if adopted, cuts off debate, and brings the assembly to a vote on the

---

* It will be noticed that the first two of these motions only close debate by virtue of their suppressing the question itself. The circumstances under which each of these motions to suppress debate and to suppress the questions should be used, are explained in § § 58, 59.

† In the U.S. House of Representatives, where each speaker can occupy the floor one hour, any of these motions to cut off debate can be adopted by a mere majority, but practically they are not used until after some debate; Rule 28, ¶ 3, H.R., expressly provides that forty minutes, twenty on each side, shall be allowed for debate whenever the previous question is ordered on a proposition on which there has been no debate, or when the rules are suspended. In ordinary societies harmony is so essential that a two-thirds vote should be required to force the assembly to a final vote without allowing free debate [see note to § 39].

pending question only, excepting where the pending motion is an amendment or a motion to commit, when it also applies to the question to be amended or committed, unless it is demanded only on the amendment or the motion to commit. When it is ordered on an amendment, or an amendment of an amendment, debate is closed and the vote taken on the amendment, when the effect of the previous question is then exhausted, and new amendments can be offered and debated.

(d) For the assembly to adopt an *order* (1) *limiting debate* upon a special subject, either as to the number or length of speeches; or (2) *closing debate* upon the subject at a stated time, when all pending questions shall be put to vote without further debate. Either of these two measures may be applied simply to a pending amendment, or an amendment thereto; and when this is voted upon, the original question is still open to debate and amendment.

Art. VI. Vote
[§§ 38, 39.]

38. Voting. Whenever from the nature of the question it permits of no modification or debate, the chairman immediately puts it to vote; if the question is debatable, when the chairman thinks the debate has been brought to a close he should inquire if the assembly is ready for the question, and if no one rises he puts the question to vote. There are various forms for putting the question in use in different parts of the country. The rule in Congress, in the House of Representatives, requires questions to be put as follows: "As many as are in favor [as the question may be] say *aye;*" and after the affirmative voice is expressed, "As many as are opposed say *no.*" The following form is very common: "It has been moved and seconded that [here state the question]; as many as are in favor of the motion say *aye;* those opposed *no.*" Or, if the motion is for adoption of a certain resolution, after it has been read the chairman can say, "You have heard the resolution read; those in favor of its adoption will hold up the right hand; those opposed will manifest it by the same sign." These examples* are sufficient to show the usual meth-

* See § 65 and also the Table of Rules, p. 14, for the forms of stating and putting certain questions.

ods of putting a question, the affirmative being always put first.

A majority vote, that is, a majority of the votes cast, ignoring blanks, is sufficient for the adoption of any motion that is in order, except those mentioned in § 39, which require a two-thirds vote. A plurality vote never adopts a motion nor elects any one except by virtue of a special rule previously adopted. [§ 39, 1st note.]

When a vote is taken the chairman should always announce the result in the following form: "The motion is carried—the resolution is adopted," or, "The ayes have it—the resolution is adopted." If, when he announces a vote, any member rises and states that he doubts the vote, or calls for a "division," the chairman shall say, "A division is called for; those in favor of the motion will rise." After counting these, and announcing the number, he shall say, "Those opposed will rise." He will count these, announce the number, and declare the result; that is, whether the motion is carried or lost. Instead of counting the vote himself, he can direct the secretary, or appoint tellers, to make the count and report to him. When tellers are appointed, they should be selected from both sides of the question. A member has the right to change his vote (when not made by ballot) before the decision of the question has been finally and conclusively pronounced by the chair, but not afterwards.

Until the negative is put, it is in order for any member, in the same manner as if the voting had not been commenced, to rise and speak, make motions for amendment or otherwise, and thus renew the debate; and this, whether the member was in the assembly room or not when the question was put and the vote partly taken. After the chairman has announced the vote, if it is found that a member has risen and addressed the chair before the negative had been put, he is entitled to be heard on the question, the same as though the vote had not been taken. In such cases the question is in the same condition as if it had never been put.

No one can vote on a question affecting himself; but if more than one name is included in the resolution (though a sense of delicacy would prevent this right being exercised, excepting when it would change the vote) all are entitled to vote; for if this were not so, a minority could control an assembly by including the names of a sufficient number in a motion, say for preferring charges against them, and suspend them, or even expel them from the assembly.*

When there is a tie vote the motion fails, unless the chairman gives his vote for the affirmative, which he is at liberty to do, as he has a right to vote whenever his vote will affect the result. Where his vote in the negative will make a tie, he can cast it and thus defeat the measure [§ 40]. In case of an Appeal [§ 14], though the question is, "Shall the decision of the chair stand as the judgment of the assembly?" a tie vote sustains the chair, upon the principle that the decision of the chair can only be reversed by a majority.

Another form of voting is by *ballot*. This method is adopted only when required by the constitution or by-laws of the assembly, or when the assembly has ordered the vote to be taken. The chairman, in such cases, appoints at least two tellers, who distribute slips of paper, upon which each member, including the chairman, writes his vote.† In voting by ballot members are not restricted to persons who have been nominated. Closing nominations prevents the public indorsement of any other candidates, but does not prevent their being voted for and being elected. When the votes are collected, they are counted by the tellers, and the results reported to the chairman, who announces it to the assembly. The chairman announces the result of the vote, in case of an election to office, in a manner similar to the following: "The whole number of votes cast is —; the number necessary for an election is —; Mr. A received —; Mr. B,—; Mr. C,—. Mr. B, having received the required number, is elected—." Where there is only one candidate for an office, and the constitution requires the vote to be by ballot, it is common to authorize the clerk to cast the vote of the assembly for such and such a person; if anyone objects, however, it is necessary to

---

* But, after charges are preferred against a member, and the assembly has ordered him to appear for trial, he is theoretically in arrest, and is deprived of all rights of membership until his case is disposed of.

† Should the chairman neglect to vote before the ballots are counted, he cannot then vote without the permission of the assembly. In ordinary assemblies ballots should be credited to the candidates for whom they were intended, whenever that can be determined, regardless of inaccuracies in writing them.

ballot in the usual way.* So, when a motion is made to make a vote unanimous, it fails if anyone objects. In counting the ballots all blanks are ignored.

The assembly can, by a majority vote, order that the vote on any question be taken by *Yeas and Nays*.† In this method of voting the chairman states both sides of the question at once; the clerk calls the roll, and each member, as his name is called, rises and answers *yes* or *no*, and the clerk reads over the names of those who answered in the affirmative, and afterwards those in the negative, that mistakes may be corrected; he then gives the number voting on each side to the chairman, who announces the result. An entry must be made in the minutes of the names of all voting in the affirmative, and also of those in the negative.

The form of putting a question upon which the vote has been ordered to be taken by yeas and nays is similar to the following: "As many as are in favor of the adoption of these resolutions will, when their names are called, answer *yes* [or *aye*]; those opposed will answer *no*." The chairman will then direct the clerk to call the roll. The negative being put at the same time as the affirmative, it is too late, after one person has answered to the roll-call, to renew the debate. After the commencement of the roll-call it is too late to ask to be excused from voting. The yeas and nays cannot be ordered in committee of the whole [§ 32.]

* It should always be remembered that this can be done only by unanimous consent, and it is doubtful whether it should ever be allowed. An election, like every other vote of the assembly, takes effect immediately unless there is a rule to the contrary.

† Taking a vote by yeas and nays, which has the effect to place on the record how each member votes, is peculiar to this country, and, while it consumes a great deal of time, is rarely useful in ordinary societies. While it can never be used to hinder business, as long as the above rule is observed, it should not be used at all in a mass meeting, or in any other assembly whose members are not responsible to a constituency. By the Constitution, one-fifth of the members present can, in either house of Congress, order a vote to be taken by yeas and nays, and, to avoid some of the resulting inconveniences, Congress has required, for instance, that the previous question shall be seconded by a majority, thus avoiding the yeas and nays until a majority are in favor of ordering the main question. In representative bodies this method of voting is very useful, especially where the proceedings are published, as it enables the people to know how their representatives voted on important measures. If there is no legal or constitional provision for the yeas and nays being ordered by a minority in a representative body, they should adopt a rule allowing the yeas and nays

39. Motions Requiring More than a Majority Vote.*

The following motions shall require a two-thirds vote for their adoption, all others requiring a majority, as the right of discussion, and the right to have the rules enforced, should not be abridged by a mere majority:

To *Amend the Rules* (requires previous notice also)	See §45
To *Suspend the Rules*	" §18
To *Make a Special Order*	" §13
To *Take up a Question out of its Proper Order*	" §13
An Objection to the Consideration of a Question†	" §15
To *Extend the Limits of Debate*	" §34
To *Close or Limit Debate*	" §37
The Previous Question	" §20

NOTE ON MOTIONS REQUIRING MORE THAN A MAJORITY VOTE.—Every motion in this list has the effect to suspend or change some rule or custom of deliberative bodies. Judging from their form, this would be true of only the first two, but a closer examination will show that the others have a similar effect.

To make a special order suspends all the rules that interfere with the consideration of the question at the specified time.

To take up a question out of its proper order is a change in the order of business.

An objection to the consideration of a question, if sustained, suspends or conflicts with the right of a member to introduce a measure to the assembly; a right which certainly has been established by custom, if it is not inherent to the very idea of a

---

to be ordered by a one-fifth vote, as in Congress, or even by a much smaller number. In some small bodies a vote on a resolution must be taken by yeas and nays, upon the demand of a single member.

---

* A two-thirds, or majority, vote means two-thirds or a majority of votes cast, ignoring blanks, which should never be counted. Sometimes By-Laws provide for a vote of two-thirds of the members present, or simply of two-thirds of the members, which may be very different from a two-thirds vote. Thus, if twelve members vote on a question in a meeting of a society where twenty are present out of a total membership of thirty, a two-thirds vote would be eight; a two-thirds vote of those present would be fourteen; and a vote of two-thirds of the members would be twenty. In this case a majority vote would be seven.

A person is said to have a *plurality* vote when he has more votes for a certain office or position than any of his rivals. In civil government, as a rule all officers elected by a popular vote are elected by a plurality. But in a deliberative assembly, where voting may be repeated until there is an election, a plurality never elects except by virtue of a special rule.

† The negative vote on considering the question must be two-thirds to dismiss the question for that session.

deliberative body. [Though Rule 41 H. R. allows a majority vote to decide this question, it is so inexpedient that the rule has not been taken advantage of lately.]

To extend the limits of debate, is to suspend a rule or an order of the assembly.

The Previous Question, and motions to *close or limit debate,* have the effect of forcing the assembly to take final action upon a question without allowing discussion; in other words, they suspend this fundamental principle of deliberative bodies, namely, that the assembly shall not be forced to final action on a question until every member has had an opportunity of discussing its merits. The very idea of a deliberative assembly is that it is a body to deliberate upon questions, and therefore members must have the right of introducing questions, and of discussing their merits, before expressing their deliberate sense upon them. [Of course, a majority can lay the question on the table, and thus stop debate; but in this case the assembly can at any time take it from the table. By this means the majority can instantly get rid of any question until they wish to consider it.]

But there are times when it is expedient to suspend these rights to introduce and debate questions, just the same as it is frequently an advantage to suspend the rules of the assembly, or to change the order of business. If, however, a bare majority could at any time suspend or change these rules and privileges, they would be of but little value. Experience has shown that a two-thirds vote should be required to adopt any motion that has the effect to suspend or change the rules or established order of business, and the rule above is made on this general principle. [The old parliamentary practice did not allow of a suspension of the rules except by unanimous consent.]

As just stated, Congress, by rule, allows a majority to sustain an objection to the consideration of a question, but the rule has very properly gone out of use. So, too, the previous question, and motions to close or limit debate, while not used in the Senate, can be adopted by a majority in the House of Representatives.

On account of the immense amount of business to be transacted during each session by the National House of Representatives, and the large number of members each one of whom is entitled to the floor in debate for one hour, it seems an absolute necessity for them to permit a majority to limit or cut off entirely the debate, and thus practically to suspend one of the fundamental rules of deliberative bodies. This is the more necessary in Congress because the party lines are strictly drawn, and the minority could almost stop legislation if they could prevent the debate from being cut off.

In all bodies situated in these respects like Congress, a rule should be adopted allowing a majority to adopt the previous question, and motions to limit or close debate. [See the last note to § 38 in reference to the yeas and nays being ordered by a one-fifth vote in Congress, and by even a smaller vote in some other bodies. The two notes in the Introduction, on pp. 19-21, may be read with advantage in connection with this note.]

Art. VII. The Officers and the Minutes
[§§ 40, 41.]

40. Chairman* or President. The presiding officer, when no special title has been assigned him, is ordinarily called the Chairman (or in religious assemblies more usually the Moderator); frequently the constitution of the assembly prescribes for him a title, such as President.

His duties are generally as follows:

To open the session at the time at which the assembly is to meet, by taking the chair and calling the members to order; to announce the business before the assembly in the order in which it is to be acted upon [§ 44]; to state and to put to vote [§§ 38, 65] all questions which are regularly moved, or necessarily arise in the course of proceedings, and to announce the result of the vote;

To restrain the members, when engaged in debate, within the rules of order;† to enforce on all occasions the observance of order and decorum [§ 36] among the members, deciding all questions of order (subject to an appeal to the assembly by any two members, § 14), and to inform the assembly when necessary, or when referred to for the purpose, on a point of order or practice.

To authenticate, by his signature, when necessary, all the acts, orders, and proceedings of the assembly, and in general to represent and stand for the assembly, declaring its will, and in all things obeying its commands.

The chairman shall rise‡ to put a question to vote, but may state it sitting; he shall also rise from his seat (without calling any one to the chair) when

---

* In connection with this section read §§ 2, 24, 44, 65.

† Should the disorder become so great that business cannot be transacted, and the chairman cannot enforce order, as a last resort he can declare the assembly adjourned.

‡ It is not customary for the chairman to rise while putting questions in very small bodies, such as committees, boards of trustees, etc.

speaking to a question of order, which he can do in preference to other members. In referring to himself he should always use his official title, thus: "The chair decides so and so," not "I decide, etc." When a member has the floor, the chairman cannot interrupt him so long as he does not transgress any of the rules of the assembly, excepting as provided in § 2.

He is entitled to vote when the vote is by ballot,* and in all other cases where the vote would change the result. Thus, in a case where a two-thirds vote is necessary, and his vote thrown with the minority would prevent the adoption of the question, he can cast his vote; so, also, he can vote with the minority when it will produce a tie vote and thus cause the motion to fail. Whenever a motion is made referring especially to the chairman, the secretary, or on his failure to do so, the maker of the motion, should put it to vote.

The chairman can, if it is necessary to vacate the chair appoint a chairman *pro tem.*,† but the first adjournment puts an end to the appointment, which the assembly can terminate before, if it pleases, by electing another chairman. But the regular chairman, knowing that he will be absent from a future meeting, cannot authorize another member to act in his place at such meeting; the clerk [§ 41], or, in his absence, any member should, in such case, call the meeting to order, and a chairman *pro tem.* be elected who would hold office during that session [§ 42], unless such office was terminated by the entrance of the regular chairman. If there are vice-presidents, the first on the list that is present takes the chair during the absence of the president.

The chairman sometimes calls a member to the chair, and himself takes part in the debate; but this should rarely be done, and nothing can justify it in a case where much feeling is shown, and there is a liability to difficulty in preserving order. If the chairman has even the appearance of being a partisan, he loses much

---

* But this right is lost if he does not use it before the tellers have commenced to count the ballots. The assembly can give leave to the chairman to vote under such circumstances.

† When there are vice-presidents, then the first one on the list that is present is, by virtue of his office, chairman during the absence of the president, and should always be called to the chair when the president temporarily vacates it.

OFFICERS AND MINUTES

of his ability to control those who are on the opposite side of the question.*

The chairman should not only be familiar with parliamentary usage, and set the example of strict conformity thereto,† but he should be a man of executive ability, capable of controlling men; and it should never be forgotten, that, to control others, it is necessary to control one's self. An excited chairman can scarcely fail to cause trouble in a meeting.

A chairman should not permit the object of a meeting to be defeated by a few factious persons using parliamentary forms with the evident object of obstructing business. In such a case he should refuse to entertain the dilatory motion, and, if an appeal is taken, he should entertain it, and, if sustained by a large majority, he can afterwards refuse to entertain even an appeal made by the faction, while they are continuing their obstruction. But the chair should never adopt such a course merely to expedite business, when the opposition is not factious. It is only justifiable when it is perfectly clear that the opposition is trying to obstruct business.

A chairman will often find himself perplexed with the difficulties attending his position, and in such cases he will do well to heed the advice of a distinguished writer on parliamentary law, and recollect that

"The great purpose of all rules and forms is to subserve the will of the assembly rather than to restrain it; to facilitate, and not to obstruct, the expression of their deliberate sense."

---

* See § 28 for duties of Chairmen of Committees.

The unfortunate habit many chairmen have of constantly speaking on questions before the assembly, even interrupting the member who has the floor, is unjustified by either the common parliamentary law or the practice of Congress. One who expects to take an active part in debate should never accept the chair.

"It is a general rule in all deliberative assemblies, that the presiding officer shall not participate in the debate, or other proceedings, in any other capacity than as such officer. He is only allowed, therefore, to state matters of fact within his knowledge; to inform the assembly on points of order or the course of proceeding, when called upon for that purpose, or when he finds it necessary to do so; and, on appeals from his decision on question of order, to address the assembly in debate." [Cushing's Manual, § 202.]

"Though the Speaker [Chairman] may of right speak to matters of order and be first heard, he is restrained from speaking on any other subject except where the assembly have occasion for facts within his knowledge; then he may, with their leave, state the matter of fact." [Jefferson's Manual, sec. xvii, and Barclay's "Digest of the Rules and Practice of the House of Representatives U.S." page 195.]

† No rules will take the place of tact and common sense on the part of

41. Clerk or Secretary *and the Minutes.* The recording officer is usually called the "Clerk" or "Secretary,"* and the record of proceedings the "Minutes." His desk should be near that of the chairman and in the absence of the chairman (if there is no vice-president present), when the hour for opening the session arrives, it is his duty to call the meeting to order, and to preside until the election of a chairman *pro tem.,* which should be done immediately. He should keep a record of the proceedings, commencing in a form similar to the following:† "At a regular quarterly meeting of [state the name of the society], held on the 31st day of March, 1875, at [state the place of meeting], the president in the chair, the minutes were read by the clerk and approved." If the regular clerk is absent, insert after the words "in the chair" the following: "The clerk being absent, Robert Smith was appointed clerk *pro tem.* The minutes were then read and approved." If the minutes were not read, say "The reading of the minutes was dispensed with." The above form will show the essentials, which are as follows: (*a*) The kind of meeting, "regular" or [stated] or "special," or "adjourned regular" or "adjourned special;" (*b*) name of

---

the chairman. While usually he need not wait for motions of routine, or for a motion to be seconded when he knows it is favored by others [see first note to § 65], yet if this is objected to, it is safer instantly to require the forms of parliamentary law to be observed. By general consent many things can be done that will save much time, but where the assembly is very large, or is divided and contains members who are continually raising points of order, the most expeditious and safe course is to enforce strictly all the rules and forms of parliamentary law.

Whenever an improper motion is made, instead of simply ruling it out of order, it is well for the chairman to suggest how the desired object can be accomplished. Thus, if it is moved "to postpone the question," he should say that if the time is not specified the proper motion is "that the question lie on the table." So, if it were moved "to lay the question on the table until a certain time," he should suggest that the proper motion is "to postpone the question to that time." Or, if it were moved to reject a resolution, he should say, "the question is on indefinitely postponing the resolution," as that is the parliamentary form of the question.

For "Hints to Inexperienced Chairmen," see § 50.

---

* When there are two secretaries, he is termed the "recording secretary," and the other one the "corresponding secretary." In many societies the secretary, besides acting as recording officer, collects the dues of members, and thus becomes to a certain extent a financial officer. In most cases the treasurer acts as banker, only paying on the order of the society, signed by the secretary alone, or by the president and secretary. In such cases the secretary becomes in reality the financial officer of the society, and should make reports to the society of funds received and from what sources, and of the funds expended and for what purposes. See § 52 for his duties as financial officer.

† See Clerk and Minutes, in Part II, § 51.

the assembly; (c) date and place of meeting (excepting when the place is always the same); (d) the fact of the presence of the regular chairman and clerk, or in their absence the names of their substitutes; (e) whether the minutes of the previous meeting were approved.

The minutes should be neatly written with ink in the record book, leaving a margin for corrections, and taken to the meetings of the society so as to be read for corrections, and approval.* After approval, however, without a reconsideration, it is in order at any future time for the society to further correct them, regardless of the time that has elapsed and the number of times they have already been amended.

The minutes should be signed by the person who acted as clerk for that meeting; in some societies the chairman must also sign them. When published, they should be signed by both officers.

In keeping the minutes, much depends upon the kind of meeting, and whether the minutes are to be published. Under no circumstances, however, should the clerk criticize in the minutes, either favorably or otherwise, anything said or done in the meeting. If they are to be published, it is often of far more interest to know what was said by the leading speakers than to know what routine business was done, and what resolutions adopted. In such cases the duties of the secretary are arduous, and he should have at least one assistant.

In ordinary society meetings and meetings of boards of managers and trustees, on the contrary, there is no object in reporting the debates; the duty of the clerk, in such cases, is mainly to record what is "done" by the assembly, not what is said by the members. Unless there is a rule to the contrary, he should enter every principal motion [§ 6] that is before the assembly, whether it is adopted or rejected; and where there is a division [see voting, § 38], or where the vote is by

---

* In many organizations it is preferable for the secretary to keep his original pencil notes in a pocket memorandum book which he carries to every meeting, and these original notes, as corrected, are approved and then copied into the permanent records. This plan results usually in neater records, but the original notes should be kept until they are carefully compared with the permanent records.

ballot, he should enter the number of votes on each side; and when the voting is by yeas and nays [§ 38], he should enter a list of the names of those voting on each side. He should indorse on the reports of committees the date of their reception, and what further action was taken upon them, and preserve them among the records, for which he is responsible. He should, in the minutes, make a brief summary of a report* that has been agreed to, except where it contains resolutions, in which case the resolutions will be entered in full as adopted by the assembly, and not as if it was the report accepted. The proceedings of the committee of the whole [§ 32], or while acting informally [§ 33], should not be entered on the minutes. Before an adjournment without day, it is customary to read over the minutes for approval, if the next meeting of the board or society will not occur for a long period. Where the regular meetings are not separated by too great a time, the minutes are read at the next meeting, and after correction should be adopted. If after their adoption errors should be detected they should be corrected regardless of the time elapsed and of the number of times the minutes have been previously corrected, and without a motion to reconsider, by a simple vote to amend the minutes.

The minutes, and all other official documents that have come before a deliberative assembly, are in the custody of the secretary. But they are open to the inspection of every member, and the chairman can even direct that certain ones be turned over to a committee that needs them for the proper performance of its duties.

The clerk should, previous to each meeting, for the use of the chairman, make out an order of business [§ 44], showing in their exact order what is necessarily to come before the assembly. He should also have, at each meeting, a list of all standing committees, and such select committees as are in existence at the time. When a committee is appointed, he should hand the names of the committee, and all papers referred to it, to the chairman of the committee, or some other of its members.

---

* If the report is of great importance the assembly should order it "to be entered on the minutes," in which case the clerk copies it in full upon the record.

Art. VIII. Miscellaneous
[§§ 42-45.]

42. A Session of an assembly is a meeting* which, though it may last for days, is virtually *one meeting,* as a session of a convention; or even months, as a session of Congress; it terminates by an "adjournment without day." The intermediate adjournments from day to day, or the recesses taken during the day, do not destroy the continuity of the meeting—they in reality constitute one session. Any meeting which is not an adjournment of another meeting commences a new session. In the case of a permanent society, having regular meetings every week, month, or year, for example, each meeting constitutes a separate session of the society, which session, however, can be prolonged by adjourning to another day.

If a principal motion [§ 6] is indefinitely postponed or rejected at one session, while it cannot be introduced again at the same session [see Renewal of a Motion, § 26], it can be at the next, unless it is prohibited by a rule of the assembly. So a question that has been laid on the table can be introduced as a new motion at any succeeding session, though it could not be done at the same session. The only way to reach it at the same session is to move to "take it from the table" [§ 19].

---

* In this Manual the term *meeting* is used to denote an assembling together of the members of a deliberative assembly for any length of time, during which there is no separation of the members by adjournment. An adjournment to meet again at some other time, even the same day, terminates the meeting, but not the session, which latter includes all the adjourned meetings. The next meeting, in this case, would be an "adjourned meeting" of the same session.

A *"meeting"* of an assembly is terminated by a temporary adjournment; a *"session"* of an assembly ends with an adjournment without day, and may consist of many meetings. Sometimes a recess is taken for a few minutes, and this does not terminate the "meeting."

In ordinary practice a meeting is closed by moving simply "to adjourn;" the society meet again at the time provided either by their rules or by a resolution of the society. If they do not meet till the time for the next regular meeting, as provided in the by-laws, then the adjournment closed the session, and was in effect an adjournment without day. If, however, they had previously fixed the time for the next meeting, either by a direct vote or by adopting a programme of exercises covering several meetings, or even days, in either case the adjournment is in effect to a certain day, and does not close the session. When an assembly has meetings several days consecutively, they all constitute one session.

No one session of the assembly can interfere with the rights of the assembly at any future session,* unless it is expressly so provided in their constitution, by-laws, or rules of order, all of which are so guarded (by requiring notice of amendments, and at least a two-thirds vote for their adoption) that they are not subject to sudden changes, but may be considered as expressing the deliberate views of the whole society, rather than the opinions or wishes of any particular meeting. Thus, if the presiding officer were ill, it would not be competent for one session of the assembly to elect a chairman to hold office longer than that session, as it cannot control or dictate to the next session of the assembly.

By going through the prescribed routine of an election to fill the vacancy, giving whatever notice is required, it could then legally elect a chairman to hold office while the vacancy lasted. So it is improper for an assembly to postpone anything to a day beyond the next succeeding session, and thus attempt to prevent the next session from considering the question. On the other hand, it is not permitted to move a reconsideration [§ 27] of a vote taken at a previous session [though the motion to reconsider can be called up, provided it was made at the last meeting of the previous session]. Committees can be appointed to report at a future session.

NOTE ON SESSION.—In Congress, and in fact all legislative bodies, the limits of the sessions are clearly defined; but in ordinary societies having a permanent existence, with regular meetings more or less frequent, there appears to be a great deal of confusion upon the subject. Any society is competent to decide what shall constitute one of its sessions, but, where there is no rule on the subject, the common parliamentary law would make each of its regular or special meetings a separate session, as they are regarded in this Manual.

The disadvantages of a rule making a session include all the meetings of an ordinary society, held during a long time, as one year, are very great. [Examine Indefinitely Postpone, § 24, and Renewal of a Motion, § 26.] If members of any society take advantage of the freedom allowed by considering each regular

---

* Any one session can adopt a rule or resolution of a permanent nature, and it continues in force until it is rescinded. But these standing rules [§ 49], as they are termed, do not interfere with future sessions, because at any moment a majority can suspend or rescind [§ 25] them, or adopt new ones.

meeting a separate session, and repeatedly renew obnoxious or unprofitable motions, the society can adopt a rule prohibiting the second introduction of any principal question [§ 6] within, say, three or six months after its rejection, or indefinite postponement, or after the society has refused to consider it. But generally it is better to suppress the motion by refusing to consider it [§ 15].

43. A Quorum of an assembly is such a number as is competent to transact its business. Unless there is a special rule on the subject, the quorum of every assembly is a majority of all the members of the assembly. But whenever a society has a permanent existence it is usual to adopt a much smaller number, the quorum being often less than one-twentieth of its members; this becomes a necessity in most large societies, where only a small fraction of the members are ever present at a meeting.*

The chairman should not take the chair till a quorum is present, except where there is no hope of there being a quorum, and then no business can be transacted, except simply to adjourn. So whenever during the meeting there is found not be a quorum present, the only thing to be done is to adjourn; though, if no question is raised about it, the debate can be continued, but no vote taken, except to adjourn.

In committee of the whole the quorum is the same as in the assembly; in any other committee the majority is a quorum, unless the assembly order otherwise, and it must wait for a quorum before proceeding to business. If the number afterwards should be reduced below a quorum, business is not interrupted, unless a member calls attention to the fact; but no question can be decided except when a quorum is present. Boards of trustees, managers, directors, etc., are on the same footing as committees, in regard to a quorum. Their power is delegated to them as a body, and their quorum, or what number shall be present, in order that

---

* While a quorum is competent to transact any business, it is usually not expedient to transact important business unless there is a fair attendance at the meeting, or else previous notice of such action has been given. Unanimous consent cannot be given when a quorum is not present.

In the English Parliament, the House of Lords, consisting of about four hundred and fifty members, can proceed to business if three members are present; and the House of Commons, with about six hundred and seventy members, requires only forty members for a quorum. The U.S. Constitution [Art. I, Sec. 5] provides that a majority of each House of Congress shall constitute a quorum to do business.

they may act as a board, is to be decided by the society that appoints the board or committee. If no quorum is specified, then it consists of a majority.*

44. Order of Business. It is customary for every society having a permanent existence to adopt an order of business for its meetings. When no rule has been adopted, the following is the order:

(1) Reading of Minutes† of the previous meeting (and their approval).
(2) Reports of Standing Committees.
(3) Reports of Select Committees.
(4) Unfinished Business.
(5) New Business.

Boards of managers, trustees, etc., come under the head of standing committees. If a subject has been made a "special order" [§ 13] for the day, it takes precedence of all business except reading the minutes. The "orders of the day" [§ 13], which include business postponed to this meeting, come in with unfinished business.

If it is desired to transact business out of its order, it is necessary to suspend the rules [§ 18], which can only be done by a two-thirds vote; but, as each resolution or report comes up, a majority can at once lay it on the table [§ 19], and thus reach any question of which they desire to first dispose.‡

45. Amendments of Rules of Order. These rules can be amended at any regular meeting of the assembly, by a two-thirds vote, provided the amendment was submitted in writing at the previous regular meeting. And no amendment to constitutions or by-laws shall be

---

* Care should be taken in amending the rule providing for a quorum. If the rule is stricken out first, then the quorum instantly becomes a majority of all the members, so that in many societies it would be nearly impracticable to secure a quorum to adopt the new rule. The proper way is to amend by striking out certain words [or the whole rule] and inserting certain other words [or the new rule], which is voted on as one question.

† It is not customary, or necessary, when several meetings are held each day, to have the minutes read more than once a day, usually at the first meeting held.

‡ It is improper to lay on the table or to postpone a class of questions, like reports of committees, or in fact anything but the question before the assembly [See § 19].

permitted, without at least equal notice and a two-thirds vote.*

---

* Constitution, by-laws, and rules of order should always prohibit their being amended by less than a two-thirds vote, and without previous notice of the amendment being given. The object of this notice is to inform the society that the subject-matter of the amendment will be up for consideration and action at a certain time. It is not to be inferred that notice is required to amend this amendment; if this were the case it would be almost impossible to properly amend by-laws, etc. But this last amendment must be germane to the original amendment; no other amendment is in order or can delay action on the original amendment. In many cases the by-laws provide that an amendment must be read at a certain number of regular meetings before being acted upon; the first reading is by the clerk when it is first proposed, and after the last reading it is up for action; so that if it has to be read at three regular meetings, in a society with regular weekly meetings, action on an amendment would be delayed for only two weeks after it was first proposed.

PART II

ORGANIZATION AND CONDUCT OF BUSINESS*

Art. IX. Organization and Meetings
[§§ 46-49.]

46. An Occasional or Mass Meeting.

(a) *Organization.* When a meeting is held, which is not one of an organized society, shortly after the time appointed for the meeting, some member of the assembly steps forward and says: "The meeting will please come to order; I move that Mr. A act as chairman of this meeting." Some one else says, "I second the motion." The first member then puts the question to vote, by saying, "It has been moved and seconded that Mr. A act as chairman of this meeting; those in favor of the motion will say *aye;*" and when the affirmative vote is taken, he says, "those opposed will say *no.*" If the majority vote is in the affirmative, he says, "The motion is carried; Mr. A will take the chair." If the motion is lost, he announces that fact, and calls for the nomination of someone else for chairman, and proceeds with the new nomination as in the first case.†

When Mr. A takes the chair he says, "The first business in order is the election of a secretary." Some one then makes a motion as just described, or he says, "I nominate Mr. B," when the chairman puts the

---

* The exact words used by the chairman or member are in many cases in quotations. It is not to be inferred that these are the only forms permitted, but that these forms are proper and common. They are inserted for the benefit of those unaccustomed to parliamentary forms, and are sufficiently numerous for ordinary meetings.

If pressed for time, the beginner, after reading this section, should begin at § 54, and read the remainder of this second part.

† Sometimes a member nominates a chairman and no vote is taken, the assembly signifying their approval by acclamation. The member who calls the meeting to order, instead of making the motion himself, may act as temporary chairman, and say: "The meeting will please come to order;

question as before. Sometimes several names are called out, and the chairman, as he hears them, says, "Mr. B is nominated; Mr. C is nominated," etc.; he then takes a vote on the first one he heard, putting the question thus: "As many as are in favor of Mr. B acting as secretary of this meeting will say *aye;* those opposed will say *no.*" If the motion is lost the question is put on Mr. C, and so on, till some one is elected. The secretary should take his seat near the chairman, and keep a record of the proceedings, as described in § 51.

(b) *Adoption of Resolutions.* These two officers are all that are usually necessary for a meeting; so, when the secretary is elected, the chairman asks, "What is the further pleasure of the meeting?" If the meeting is merely a public assembly called together to consider some special subject, it is customary at this stage of the proceedings for some one to offer a series of resolutions previously prepared, or else to move the appointment of a committee to prepare resolutions upon the subject. In the first case he rises and says, "Mr. Chairman;" the chairman responds, "Mr. C." Mr. C having thus obtained the floor, then says, "I move the adoption of the following resolutions," which he then reads and hands to the chairman;* some one else says, "I second the motion." The chairman sometimes directs the secretary to read the resolutions again, after which he says, "The question is on the adoption of the resolutions just read," and if no one rises immediately, he adds, "Are you ready for the question?" if no one then rises, he says, "As many as are in favor of the adoption of the resolutions just

---

will some one nominate a chairman?" He puts the question to vote on the nomination as described above. In large assemblies, the member who nominates, with one other member, frequently conducts the presiding officer to the chair, and the chairman makes a short speech, thanking the assembly for the honor conferred on him.

---

* The practice, in legislative bodies, is to send to the clerk's desk all resolutions, bills, etc., the title of the bill and the name of the member introducing it being indorsed on each. In such bodies, however, there are several clerks and only one chairman. In many assemblies there is but one clerk or secretary, and as he has to keep the minutes there is no reason for his being constantly interrupted to read every resolution offered. In such assemblies, unless there is a rule or established custom to the contrary, it is allowable and frequently much better, to hand all resolutions, reports, etc., directly to the chairman. If they were read by the member introducing them, and no one calls for another reading, the chairman can omit reading them when he thinks they are fully understood. For the manner of reading and stating the question, when the resolution contains several paragraphs, see § 44.

read will say *aye;*" after the ayes have voted, he says, "As many as are of a contrary opinion will say *"no;"* he then announces the result of the vote as follows: "The motion is carried—the resolutions are adopted," or, "The ayes have it—the resolutions are adopted."

(c) *Committee to draft Resolutions.* If it is preferred to appoint a committee to draft resolutions, a member, after he has addressed the chair and been recognized, says: "I move that a committee be appointed to draft resolutions expressive of the sense of this meeting on," etc., adding the subject for which the meeting was called. This motion being seconded, the chairman states the question [§ 65] and asks: "Are you ready for the question?" If no one rises he puts the question, and announces the result; and if it is carried, he asks: "Of how many shall the committee consist?" If only one number is suggested, he announces that the committee will consist of that number; if several numbers are suggested, he states the different ones and then takes a vote on each, beginning with the largest, until one number is selected.

He then inquires: "How shall the committee be appointed?" This is usually decided without the formality of a vote. The committee may be "appointed" by the chair, in which case the chairman names the committee, and no vote is taken; or the committee may be "nominated" by the chair, or the members of the assembly (no member naming more than one, except by unanimous consent), and then the assembly vote on their appointment. When the chairman nominates, after stating the names he puts one question on the entire committee, thus: "As many as are in favor of these gentlemen constituting the committee will say *aye.*" If nominations are made by members of the assembly, and more names mentioned than the number of the committee, a separate vote should be taken on each name. (In a mass meeting it is safer to have all committees appointed by the chairman.)

When the committee are appointed they should at once retire and agree upon a report, which should be written out as described in § 53. During their absence other business may be attended to, or the time may be occupied with hearing addresses. Upon their return*

---

* If the chairman sees the committee return to the room, he should, as soon as the member speaking closes, announce that the assembly will

the chairman of the committee (who is the first named on the committee, and who quite commonly, though not necessarily, is the one who made the motion to appoint the committee), avails himself of the first opportunity to obtain the floor [see § 2], when he says: "The committee appointed to draft resolutions are prepared to report." The chairman tells him that the assembly will now hear the report, which is then read by the chairman of the committee and handed to the presiding officer, upon which the committee is dissolved without any action of the assembly.

A member then moves the "adoption" or "acceptance" of the report, or that "the resolutions be agreed to," which motions have the same effect if carried, namely, to make the resolutions the resolutions of the assembly, just as if the committee had had nothing to do with them.* When one of these motions is made the chairman acts as stated above, when the resolutions were offered by a member. If it is not desired immediately to adopt the resolutions, they can be debated, modified, their consideration postponed, etc., as explained in §§ 55-63.

When through with the business for which the assembly was convened, or when from any other cause it is desirable to close the meeting, some one moves "to adjourn;" if the motion is carried, and no other time for meeting has been appointed, the chairman says: "The motion is carried; this assembly stands adjourned without day." [Another method by which the meeting may be conducted is shown in § 48.]

(d) *Additional Officers.* If more officers are required than a chairman and secretary, they can be appointed before introducing the resolutions in the manner described for those officers; or, the assembly can first form a temporary organization in the manner already described, only adding "pro tem." to the title of the officers, thus, "chairman pro tem." In this latter case, as soon as the secretary pro tem. is elected, a committee is appointed to nominate the permanent officers, as in the case of a convention [§ 47]. Frequently the presiding officer is called the President, and sometimes there is a large number of Vice-Presidents appointed for mere

---

now hear the report of the committee on resolutions; or before this announcement he may ask if the committee is prepared to report.

* See note to § 80 for some common errors in acting upon reports.

complimentary purposes. The Vice-Presidents in large formal meetings sit on the platform beside the President, and in his absence, or when he vacates the chair, the first on the list that is present should take the chair.

47. Meeting of a Convention or Assembly of Delegates. If the members of the assembly have been elected or appointed as members, it becomes necessary to know who are properly members of the assembly and entitled to vote, before the permanent organization is effected. In this case a temporary organization* is made, as already described, by the election of a chairman and secretary "pro-tem.," when the chairman announces, "The next business in order is the appointment of a committee on credentials." A motion may then be made covering the entire case, thus: "I move that a committee of three on the credentials of members be appointed by the chair, and that the committee report as soon as practicable;" or they may include only one of these details, thus: "I move that a committee be appointed on the credentials of members." In either case the chair proceeds as already described in the cases of committees on resolutions [§ 46 (c)].

On the motion to accept the report of the committee, none can vote except those reported by the committee as having proper credentials. The committee, beside reporting a list of members with proper credentials, may report doubtful or contested cases, with recommendations, which the assembly may adopt, or reject, or postpone, etc. Only members whose right to their seats is undisputed can vote.

The chairman, after the question of credentials is disposed of, at least for the time, announces that "The next business in order is the election of permanent officers of the assembly." Some one then moves the appointment of a committee to nominate the officers, in a form similar to this: "I move that a committee of three be appointed by the chair to nominate permanent officers of this convention." This motion is treated as already explained. When the committee makes its report, some one moves "that the report of the com-

---

* Care should be taken to put no one into office, or on a committee, whose right to a seat is doubted.

mittee be accepted, and that the officers nominated be declared the officers of this convention."* This motion being carried, the chairman declares the officers elected, and instantly calls the new presiding officer to the chair, and the temporary secretary is at the same time replaced. The convention is now organized for work.

48. A Permanent Society. (a) *First Meeting.* When it is desired to form a permanent society, those interested in it should see that only the proper persons are invited to be present at a certain time and place. It is not usual in mass meetings or meetings called to organize a society, to commence until ten or fifteen minutes after the appointed time, when some one steps forward and says: "The meeting will please come to order; I move that Mr. A act as chairman of this meeting." Some one "seconds the motion," when the one who made the motion puts it to vote (or, as it is called, "puts the question"), as already described under an "occasional meeting" [§ 46 (a)]; and, as in that case, when the chairman is elected he announces as the first business in order, the election of a secretary.

After the secretary is elected, the chairman calls on some member who is most interested in getting up the society to state the object of the meeting. When this member rises he says: "Mr. Chairman." The chairman then announces his name, when the member proceeds to state the object of the meeting. Having finished his remarks, the chairman may call on other members to give their opinions upon the subject, and sometimes a particular speaker is called out by members who wish to hear him. The chairman should observe the wishes of the assembly, and, while being careful not to be too strict, he must not permit any one to occupy too much time and weary the meeting.

When a sufficient time has been spent in this informal way, some one should offer a resolution, so that definite action can be taken. Those interested in getting up the meeting, if it is to be a large one, should have

---

* Where there is any competition for the offices, it is better that they be elected by ballot. In this case, when the nominating committee report, a motion can be made as follows: "I move that the convention now proceed to ballot for its permanent officers ;" or, "I move that we now proceed to the election, by ballot, of the permanent officers of this convention." [See § 38 for balloting and other methods of voting.] The constitutions of permanent societies usually provide that the officers shall be elected by ballot.

previously agreed upon what is to be done, and be prepared, at the proper time, to offer a suitable resolution, which may be in form similar to this: "Resolved, That it is the sense of this meeting that a society for [state the object of the society] should now be formed in this city." This resolution, when seconded and stated by the chairman, would be open to debate, and be treated as already described [§ 46 (b)]. This preliminary motion could have been offered at the commencement of the meeting, and, if the meeting is a very large one, this would generally be better than to have the informal discussion.

After this preliminary motion has been voted on, or even without waiting for such motion, one like this can be offered: "I move that a committee of five be appointed by the chair to draft a constitution and by-laws for a society for [here state the object], and that they report at an adjourned meeting of this assembly. This motion can be amended [§ 56] by striking out and adding words, etc., and it is debatable.

When this committee is appointed, the chairman may inquire: "Is there any other business to be attended to?" or, "What is the further pleasure of the meeting?" When all business is finished, a motion can be made to adjourn, to meet at a certain place and time, which, when seconded and stated by the chair, is open to debate and amendment. It is usually better to fix the time of the next meeting [see § 63] at an earlier stage of the meeting; and then, when it is desired to close the meeting, move simply "to adjourn," which cannot be amended or debated. When this motion is carried, the chairman says: "This meeting stands adjourned, to meet at," etc., specifying the time and place of the next meeting.

(b) *Second Meeting.** At the next meeting the officers of the previous meeting, if present, serve until the permanent officers are elected. When the hour

---

* Ordinary meetings of a society are conducted like this second meeting, the chairman, however, announcing the business in the order prescribed by the rules of the society [§ 44]. For example, after the minutes are read and approved, he would say, "The next business in order is hearing the reports from the standing committees." He may then call upon each committee in their order for a report, thus: "Has the committee on applications for membership any report to make?" In which case the committee may report, as shown above, or some member of it reply that they have no report to make. Or, when the chairman knows that there are but few if any reports to make, it is better, after making the announcement of the

arrives for the meeting, the chairman standing, says, "The meeting will please come to order;" as soon as the assembly is seated, he adds, "The secretary will read the minutes of the last meeting." If any one notices an error in the minutes, he can state the fact as soon as the secretary finishes reading them; if there is no objection, without waiting for a motion, the chairman directs the secretary to make the correction. The chairman then says, "If there is no objection the minutes will stand approved as read" [or "corrected," if any corrections have been made].

He announces as the next business in order, "the hearing of the report of the committee on the Constitution and By-Laws," The chairman of the committee, after addressing "Mr. Chairman" and being recognized, reads the committee's report and then hands it to the chairman.* If no motion is made, the chairman says, "You have heard the report read—what order shall be taken upon it?" Or simply inquires "What shall be done with the report?" Some one moves its adoption, or still better, moves "the adoption of the constitution reported by the committee, and when seconded, the chairman says, "The question is on the adoption of the constitution reported by the committee." He then reads the first article of the constitution, and asks, "Are there any amendments proposed to this article?" If none are offered, after a pause, he reads the next article, and asks the same question, and proceeds thus until he reads the last article, when he says, "The whole constitution having been read, it is open to amendment." Now any one can move amendments to any part of the constitution.

When the chairman thinks it has been modified to suit the wishes of the assembly, he inquires: "Are you ready for the question?" If no one wishes to speak, he puts the question: "As many as are in favor of adopting

---

business, for him to ask, "Have these committees any reports to make?" After a short pause, if no one rises to report, he states, "There being no reports from the standing committees, the next business in order is hearing the reports of select committees," when he will act the same as in the case of the standing committees. The chairman should always have a list of the committees, to enable him to call upon them, as well as to guide him in the appointment of new committees.

---

* In large and formal bodies the chairman, before inquiring what is to be done with the report, usually directs the secretary to read it again. See note to § 30 for a few common errors in acting upon reports of committees. [See also note to § 46 (b).]

the constitution as amended will say *aye;*" and then, "As many as are opposed will say *no.*" He distinctly announces the result of the vote, which should always be done. If the articles of the constitution are subdivided into sections or paragraphs, then the amendments should be made by sections or paragraphs, instead of by articles.

The chairman now states that the constitution having been adopted, it will be necessary for those wishing to become members to sign it (and pay the initiation fee, if required by the constitution), and suggests, if the assembly is a large one, that a recess be taken for the purpose. A motion is then made to take a recess for say ten minutes, or until the constitution is signed. The constitution being signed, no one is permitted to vote excepting those who have signed it.

The recess having expired, the chairman calls the meeting to order, and says: "The next business in order is the adoption of by-laws." Some one moves the adoption of the by-laws reported by the committee, and they are treated just like the constitution. The chairman then asks: "What is the further pleasure of the meeting?" or states that the next business in order is the election of the permanent officers of the society. In either case some one moves the appointment of a committee to nominate the permanent officers of the society, which motion is treated as already described in § 47. As each officer is elected he replaces the temporary one, and when they are all elected the organization is completed.

If the society is one that expects to own real estate, it should be incorporated according to the laws of the State in which it is situated, and for this purpose some one on the committee on the constitution should consult a lawyer before this second meeting, so that the constitution may conform to the laws. In this case the trustees are usually instructed to take the proper measures to have the society incorporated.

49. Constitutions, By-Laws, Rules of Order, and Standing Rules. In forming a constitution and by-laws it is always best to procure copies of those adopted by several similar societies, and for the committee, after comparing them, to select one as the basis of their own, amending each article just as their own report is amended by the society. When they have completed

ORGANIZATION AND MEETINGS

amending the constitution it is adopted by the committee. The by-laws are treated in the same way; and then, having finished the work assigned them, some one moves "that the committee rise, and that the chairman (or some other member) report the constitution and by-laws to the assembly." If this is adopted, the constitution and by-laws are written out, and a brief report made of this form: "Your committee, appointed to draft a constitution and by-laws, would respectfully submit the following, with the recommendation that they be adopted as the constitution and by-laws of this society," which is signed by all the members of the committee that concur in it. Sometimes the report is only signed by the chairman of the committee.

In the organization just given it is assumed that both a constitution and by-laws are adopted. This is not always done; some societies adopt only a constitution, and others only by-laws. When both are adopted, the *Constitution* usually contains only the following:

(1) Name and object of the society.

(2) Qualification of members.

(3) Officers, their election and duties.

(4) Meetings of the society (only including what is essential, leaving details to the by-laws).

(5) How to amend the constitution.

These can be arranged in five articles, each article being subdivided into sections. The constitution containing nothing but what is fundamental, it should be made very difficult to amend; usually, previous notice of the amendment is required, and also a two-thirds or three-fourths vote for its adoption [§ 45]. It is better not to require a larger vote than two-thirds; and, where the meetings are frequent, an amendment should not be allowed to be made except at a quarterly or annual meeting, after having been proposed at the previous quarterly meeting.

The *By-Laws* contain all the other standing rules of the society, of such importance that they should be placed out of the power of any one meeting to modify; or they may omit the rules relating to the conduct of business in the meetings, which would then constitute the *Rules of Order* of the society. Every society, in its by-laws or rules of order, should adopt a rule like this: "The rules contained in [specifying the work on parliamentary practice] shall govern the society in all cases to which they are applicable, and in which they are not inconsistent with the rules of order (or by-laws) of this society." Without such a rule, any one so disposed could cause great trouble in a meeting.

In addition to the constitution, by-laws, and rules of order, in nearly every society resolutions of a permanent nature are occasionally adopted, which are binding on the society until they are rescinded or modified. These are called *Standing Rules,* and can be adopted by a majority vote at any meeting. After they have been adopted, they cannot be modified at the same session except by a reconsideration [§ 60]. At any future session they can be suspended, modified, or rescinded by a majority vote. The standing rules, then, comprise those rules of a society which have been adopted like ordinary resolutions, without the previous notice, etc., required for by-laws, and, consequently future sessions of the society are at liberty to terminate them whenever they please. No standing rule (or other resolution) can be adopted which conflicts with the constitution, by-laws, or rules of order.*

Art. X. Officers and Committees

50. Chairman or President. It is the duty of the chairman to call the meeting to order at the appointed time, to preside at all the meetings, to announce the business before the assembly in its proper order, to state and put all questions properly brought before the assembly, to preserve order and decorum, and to decide all questions of order (subject to an appeal). When he "puts a question" to vote, and when speaking upon an appeal, he

---

* In practice these various classes of rules are frequently very much mixed. The standing rules of some societies are really by-laws, as the society cannot suspend them, nor can they be amended until previous notice is given. This produces confusion without any corresponding benefit.

Standing Rules should contain only such rules as are subject to the will of the majority of any meeting, and which it may be expedient to change at any time, without the delay incident to giving previous notice. *Rules of Order* should contain only the rules relating to the orderly transaction of the business in the meetings of the society. The *By-Laws* should contain all the other rules of the society which are of too great importance to be changed without giving notice to the society of such change; provided that the most important of these can be placed in a *Constitution* instead of in the by-laws. These latter three should provide for their amendment. The rules of order should provide for their suspension. The by-laws sometimes provide for the suspension of certain articles [see note to § 18.]

should stand;* in all other cases he can sit. In all cases where his vote would affect the result, or where the vote is by ballot, he can vote. When a member rises to speak, he should say, "Mr. Chairman," and the chairman should reply, "Mr. A;" he should not interrupt a speaker so long as he is in order, but should listen to his speech, which should be addressed to him and not to the assembly. The chairman should be careful to abstain from the appearance of partisanship, but he has the right to call another member to the chair while he addresses the assembly on a question; when speaking to a question or order he does not leave the chair.

HINTS TO INEXPERIENCED CHAIRMEN.—While in the chair, have beside you your Constitution, By-Laws and Rules of Order, which should be studied until you are perfectly familiar with them. You cannot tell the moment you may need this knowledge. If a member asks what motion to make in order to attain a certain object, you should be able to tell him at once. [See § 55.] You should memorize the list of ordinary motions arranged in their order of precedence [see page 14], and should be able to refer to the Table of Rules so quickly that there would be no delay in deciding all points contained in it.

You should know all the business to come regularly before the meeting, and call for it in its regular order. Have with you a list of members of all committees, to guide you in nominating new committees.

As soon as a motion is made and seconded, distinctly announce what question is before the assembly; so, when a vote is taken, announce the result and also what question, if any, is then pending. [See § 54 for the proper forms.] Never wait for mere routine motions to be seconded, when you know no one objects to them. [See § 65.]

If a member ignorantly makes an improper motion, politely suggest the proper one. If it is moved "to lay the question on the table until a certain time," as the motion is improper, ask if the intention is "to postpone the question to that time"; if the answer is yes, then state that the question is on the postponement to that time. If it is moved simply "to postpone the question" without stating a time, do not rule it out of order, but ask the mover if he wishes "to postpone the question indefinitely" (which kills it), or "to lay it on the table" (which enables it to be taken up at any other time); then state the question in accordance with the motion he intended to make. So if, after a report has been presented and read, a member

---

* In meetings of boards of managers, committees, and other small bodies, the chairman usually retains his seat, and even members in speaking do not rise.

moves that "it be received," ask him if he means to move "its adoption" [or "acceptance," which is the same thing], as the report has been already received. [No vote should be taken on receiving a report, which merely brings it before the assembly and allows it to be read, unless someone objects to its reception. See note § 30.]

The chairman of a committee usually has the most to say in reference to questions before the committee; but the chairman of an ordinary deliberative assembly, especially a large one, should, of all the members, have the least to say upon the merits of pending questions.

Never interrupt members while speaking, simply because you know more about the matter than they do; never get excited; never be unjust to the most troublesome member, nor take advantage of his ignorance of parliamentary law, even though a temporary good is accomplished thereby.

Know all about parliamentary law, but do not try to show off your knowledge. Never be technical, nor be any more strict than is absolutely necessary for the good of the meeting. Use your judgment; the assembly may be of such a nature through its ignorance of parliamentary usages and peaceable disposition, that a strict enforcement of the rules, instead of assisting, would greatly hinder business; but in large assemblies, where there is much work to be done, and especially where there is liability to trouble, the only safe course is to require a strict observance of the rules.

51. The Clerk, Secretary, or Recording Secretary, as he is variously called, should keep a record of the proceedings, the character of which depends upon the kind of meeting. In an occasional or mass meeting, the record usually amounts to nothing, but he should always record every resolution or motion that is adopted.

In a convention it is often desirable to keep a full record for publication, and where it lasts for several days, it is usual, and generally best, to appoint one or more assistant clerks. Frequently it is a tax on the judgment of the clerk to decide what to enter on the record, or the "Minutes," as it is usually called. Sometimes the points of each speech should be entered, and at other times only the remark that the question was discussed by Messrs. A, B, and C in the affirmative, and Messrs. D, E, and F in the negative. Every resolution that is adopted should be entered, which can be done in this form: "On motion of Mr. D it was resolved that, etc."

Sometimes a convention does its work by having

certain topics previously assigned to certain speakers, who deliver formal addresses or essays, the subjects of which are afterwards open for discussion in short speeches—of five minutes, for instance. In such cases the minutes are very brief, unless they are to be published, when they should contain either the entire addresses, or carefully prepared abstracts of them, and should show the drift of the discussion that followed each one. In permanent societies, where the minutes are not published, they consist of a record of what was done and not what was said, and should be kept in a book. The secretary should never make in the minutes any criticism, either favorable or otherwise, upon anything said or done in a meeting.

The *Form* of the *Minutes* can be as follows:

At a regular meeting of the M. L. Society, held in their hall, on Thursday evening, March 16, 1875, Mr. A in the chair, and Mr. B acting as secretary, the minutes of the previous meeting were read and approved. The committee on Applications reported the names of Messrs. C and D as applicants for membership, and on motion of Mr. F they were admitted as members. The committee on ———— reported through Mr. G a series of resolutions, which were thoroughly discussed and amended, and finally adopted, as follows:

Resolved, That   *   *   *   *   *
*   *   *   *   *

On motion of Mr. L the society adjourned.

L———— B————,
Secretary.

If the proceedings are to be published, the secretary should always examine the published proceedings of similar meetings, so as to conform to the custom, excepting where it is manifestly improper.

The constitution, by-laws, rules of order, and standing rules should all be written in one book, leaving every other page blank; and whenever an amendment is made to any of them, it should be immediately entered on the page opposite to the article amended, with a reference to the date and page of the minutes where is recorded the action of the society.

The secretary has the custody of all papers belonging to the society, not especially under charge of any other officer. Sometimes his duties are also of a financial kind, when he should make such reports as are prescribed in the next section.

52. Treasurer. The duties of this officer vary in different societies. In probably the majority of cases he acts as a banker, merely holding the funds deposited with him, and paying them out on the order of the society signed by the secretary. His annual report, which is always required, in this case consists of merely a statement of the amount on hand at the commencement of the year, the amount received during the year (stating from what sources received), the total amount paid out by order of the society, and the balance on hand. When this report is presented it is referred to an "auditing committee," consisting of one or two persons, who examine the treasurer's books and vouchers, and certify on his report that they "have examined his accounts and vouchers and find them correct, and the balance on hand is," etc., stating the amount on hand. The auditing committee's report being accepted is equivalent to a resolution of the society to the same effect, namely, that the treasurer's report is correct.

In the case here supposed the real financial statement is made either by the board of trustees, or by the secretary or some other officer, according to the constitution of the society. The principles involved are, that every officer who receives money is to account for it in a report to the society, and that whatever officer is responsible for the disbursements shall report them to the society. If the secretary, as in many societies, is really responsible for the expenses, the treasurer merely paying upon his order, then the secretary should make a full report of these expenses, so classified as to enable the society to readily see the amounts expended for various purposes.

It should always be remembered that the financial report is made for the information of members. The details of dates and separate payments for the same object are a hindrance to its being understood, and are useless, as it is the duty of the auditing committee to examine into the details and see if the report is correct.

Every disbursing officer should be careful to get a receipt whenever he makes a payment; these receipts should be preserved in regular order, as they are the vouchers for the payments, which must be examined by the auditing committee. Disbursing officers cannot be too careful in keeping their accounts, and they should insist upon having their accounts audited every time they make a report, as by this means any error is quickly detected and may be corrected. When the society has accepted the auditing committee's report that the financial report is correct, the disbursing officer is relieved from the responsibility of the past, and if his vouchers were lost afterwards it would cause no trouble. The best form for these financial reports depends upon the kind of society, and is best determined by examining those made in similar societies.

The following form can be varied to suit most cases [when the statement of receipts and expenses is very long, it is often desirable to specify the amounts received from one or two particular sources, which can be done immediately after stating the total receipts; the same course can be taken in regard to the expenditures]:

Treasurer's Report.

The undersigned, Treasurer of the M. L. Society, begs leave to submit the following annual report:

The balance on hand at the commencement of the year was _____ dollars and _____ cents. There was received from all sources during the year _____ dollars and _____ cents; during the same time the expenses amounted to _____ dollars and _____ cents, leaving a balance on hand of _____ dollars and _____ cents.

The annexed statement of receipts and expenditures will show in detail the sources from which the receipts were obtained, and the objects to which the expenditures have been applied.

All of which is respectfully submitted.

S—— M——
Treasurer M. L. S.

The "statement of receipts and expenditures" can be made by simply giving a list of receipts, followed by a list of expenses, and finishing up with the balance on hand. The auditing committee's certificate to the correctness of the account should be written on the statement. Often the statement is made out in the form of an account, as follows:

Dr.	The M. L. S. in acct. with S. M., Treas.	Cr:
1875.		1875.
Dec. 31. To rent of hall ____$500.00		Jan. 1. By bal. on hand from
" gas _____ 80.00		last year's account $ 21.13
" stationery _____ 26.50		Dec. 31. By initiation fees __ 95.00
" janitor _____ 360.00		" members dues ___ 860.00
" balance on hand 24.63		" fines _____ 15.00
$991.13		$991.13

We do hereby certify that we have examined the accounts and vouchers of the treasurer, and find them correct; and that the balance in his hands is twenty-four dollars and sixty-three cents.

R. V.,
J. L., } *Audit Com.*

53. Committees. In small assemblies, especially in those where but little business is done, there is not much need of committees. But in large assemblies, or in those doing a great deal of business, committees are of the utmost importance. When a committee is properly selected, in nine cases out of ten its action decides that of the assembly. A committee for *action* should be small, and consist only of those heartily in favor of the proposed action. A committee for deliberation or investigation, on the contrary, should be larger, and represent all parties in the assembly, so that its opinion will carry with it as great weight as possible. The usefulness of the committee will be greatly impaired if any important faction of the assembly be unrepresented on the committee. The appointment of a committee is fully explained in § 46 (c).

The first member named on a committee is its chairman, and it is his duty to call together the committee and preside at its meetings, unless the committee by a majority of its number elects another chairman, which it is competent to do, unless the assembly has appointed the chairman. If he is absent, or from any cause fails or declines to call a meeting, it is the duty of the committee to assemble on the call of any two of its members. The committee is a miniature assembly, being able to act only when a quorum is present. If a paper is referred to them, they must not deface it in any way, but write their amendments on a separate sheet. If they originate the paper, all amendments must be incorporated in it. When they originate the paper, usually one member has previously prepared a draft, which is read entirely through, and then read by paragraphs, the chairman pausing after each paragraph, and asking: "Are there any amendments proposed to this paragraph?" No vote is taken on the adoption of the separate paragraphs; but, after the whole paper has been read in this way, it is open to amendment generally by striking out any paragraph or inserting new ones, or by substituting an entirely new paper for it. When it has been amended to suit the committee, they should adopt it as their report, and direct the chairman or some other member to report it to the assembly. It is then written out, usually commencing in a style similar to this: "The committee to which was referred [state the matter referred], beg leave to submit the following report;" or, "Your committee appointed to [specify the object], would respectfully report," etc. It usually closes thus: "All of which is respectfully submitted," followed by the signatures of all the members concurring in the report, or sometimes by only that of the chairman.

If the minority submit a report, it commences thus: "The undersigned, a minority of the committee appointed," etc., continuing as the regular report of the committee. After the committee's report has been read it is usual to allow the minority to present their report; but it cannot be acted upon except by a motion to substitute it for the report of the committee. When the committee's report is read they are discharged without any motion. A motion to refer the paper back to the same committee (or to recommit), if adopted, revives the committee.

Art. XI. Introduction of Business

54. Any member wishing to bring business before the assembly should, unless it is very simple, write down, in the form of a motion, what he would like to have the assembly adopt, thus:

Resolved, That the thanks of this convention be tendered to the citizens of this community for their hearty welcome and generous hospitality.

When there is no other business before the assembly, he rises and addresses the chairman by his title, thus: "Mr. Chairman," who immediately recognizes him by announcing his name.* He then, having the floor, says,

---

* If the chairman has any special title (as President, for instance), he should be addressed by it, thus: "Mr. President." Sometimes the chairman recognizes the speaker by merely bowing to him, but the proper course is to announce his name.

"I move the adoption of the following resolution," which he reads and hands to the chairman.* Some one else seconds the motion, and the chairman says, "It has been moved and seconded that the following resolution be adopted," when he reads the resolution; or he may read the resolution and then state the question thus: "The question is on the adoption of the resolution just read." The merits of the resolution are then open to discussion, but before any member can discuss the question or make any motion, he must first obtain the floor as just described. After the chairman states the question, if no one rises to speak, or when he thinks the debate closed, he asks, "Are you ready for the question?"† If no one then rises, he puts the question in a form similar to the following: "The question is on the adoption of the resolution which you have heard read; as many as are in favor of its adoption will say *aye*." When the ayes have voted, he says, "As many as are of a contrary opinion will say *no*." He then announces the result, stating that the motion is carried, or lost, as the case may be, in the following form: "The motion is carried —the resolution is adopted;" or, "The ayes have it,—the resolution is adopted." A majority of the votes cast is sufficient for the adoption of any motion, excepting those mentioned in § 39. [For other forms of stating and putting questions see § 65. For other illustrations of the common practice in introducing business, and in making various motions see §§ 46-48.]

Art. XII. Motions

55. Motions Classified According to their Object. Instead of immediately adopting or rejecting a resolution as originally submitted, it may be desirable to dispose of it in some other way, and for this purpose various motions have come into use, which can be made while a resolution is being considered, and, for the time being, supersede it. No one can make any of these motions while another member has the floor, excepting as shown in the Table of Rules: the circumstances under which

---

* Or, when he is recognized by the chair, he may say that he wishes to offer the following resolutions, which he reads and then moves their adoption. In very large bodies the name of the mover should be indorsed on the written resolutions, especially if much business is to be transacted.

† See second note to § 65.

each motion can be made are shown in the Order of Precedence of Motions, p. 14.

When a motion has been recognized by the chair as pending it must, if not withdrawn, be disposed of by a vote unless the meeting adjourn while it is pending. It may be interrupted by motions having precedence of it, but as soon as they are acted on, if this action does not dispose of the original question, then the consideration of that question is resumed without any new motion being made.

The following list comprises most of these motions, arranged in eight classes, according to the object for which each motion is used:

MOTIONS CLASSIFIED ACCORDING TO THEIR OBJECT.

[The object to be attained is printed thus: "(2) To defer action;" the motions to accomplish this object are printed in *Italics* under the object, and marked (a), (b) etc.; the difference in the use of these motions is shown in the section referred to.]

(1) To Modify or Amend _____[§ 56]
    (a) *Amend.*
    (b) *Commit or Refer.*

(2) To Defer Action _____[§ 57]
    (a) *Postpone to a Certain Time.*
    (b) *Lay on the Table.*

(3) To Suppress Debate _____[§ 58]
    (a) *Previous Question.*
    (b) *An Order Limiting or Closing Debate.*

(4) To Suppress the Question _____[§ 59]
    (a) *Objection to its Consideration.*
    (b) *Postpone Indefinitely.*
    (c) *Lay on the Table.*

(5) To Consider a Question the Second Time____[§ 60]
    (a) *Reconsider.*

(6) Order and Rules _____[§ 61]
    (a) *Orders of the Day.*
    (b) *Special Orders.*
    (o) *Suspension of the Rules.*
    (d) *Questions of Order.*
    (e) *Appeal.*

(7) Miscellaneous _____[§ 62]
    (a) *Reading of Papers.*
    (b) *Withdrawal of a Motion.*
    (c) *Questions of Privilege.*

(8) To Close a Meeting _____[§ 63]
    (a) *Fix the Time to which to Adjourn.*
    (b) *Adjourn.*

56. To Modify or Amend. (a) *Amend.* If it is desired to modify the question in any way, the proper motion to make is "to amend," either by "adding" words, or by "striking out" words; or by "striking out certain words and inserting others;" or by "substituting" a different motion on the same subject for the one before the assembly; or by "dividing the question" into two or more questions, as the mover specifies, so as to get a separate vote on any particular point or points. Sometimes the enemies of a measure seek to amend it in such a way as to divide its friends, and thus defeat it.

When the amendment has been moved and seconded, the chairman should always state the question distinctly, so that every one may know exactly what is before them, reading first the paragraph which it is proposed to amend; then the words to be struck out, if there are any; next, the words to be inserted, if any; and finally, the paragraph as it will stand if the amendment is adopted. He then states that the question is on the adoption of the amendment, which is open to debate, the remarks being confined to the merits of the amendment, only going into the main question so far as is necessary in order to ascertain the propriety of adopting the amendment.

This amendment can be amended, but an "amendment of an amendment" cannot be amended. None of the undebatable motions mentioned in § 35, except to fix the time to which to adjourn, to extend the limits of debate, and to close or limit debate, can be amended, nor can the motion to postpone indefinitely.

(b) *Commit or Refer.* If the original question is not well digested, or needs more amendment than can well be made in the assembly, it is usual to move "to refer it to a committee." This motion can be made while an amendment is pending, and it opens the whole merits of the question to debate. This motion can be amended by specifying the number of the committee, or how they shall be appointed, or when they shall report, or by giving them any other instructions. [See § 53 on committees, and §46 (c) on their appointment.]

57. To Defer Action. (a) *Postpone to a Certain Time.* If it is desired to defer action upon a question till a particular time, the proper motion to make is "to postpone it to that time." This motion allows of but limited

MOTIONS

debate, which must be confined to the propriety of the postponement to that time; it can be amended by altering the time, and this amendment allows of the same debate. The time specified must not be beyond that session [§ 42] of the assembly, except it be the next session, in which case it comes up with the unfinished business at the next session. This motion can be made when a motion to amend, or to commit, or to postpone indefinitely, is pending.

(b) *Lay on the Table.* Instead of postponing a question to a particular time, it may be desired to lay it aside temporarily until some other question is disposed of, retaining the privilege of resuming its consideration at any time.* The only way to accomplish this is to move that the question "lie on the table." This motion allowing of neither debate nor amendment, the chairman immediately puts the question; if carried, the whole matter is laid aside till the assembly vote to "take it from the table" (which latter motion is undebatable and possesses no privilege). Sometimes this motion is used to suppress a measure, as shown in § 59 (c).

58. To Suppress Debate.†   (a) *Previous Question.* While, as a general rule, free debate is allowed upon every motion,‡ which, if adopted, has the effect of adopting the original question or removing it from before the assembly for the session, yet, to prevent a minority from making an improper use of this privilege, it is necessary to have methods by which debate can be closed and final action can at once be taken upon a question.

To accomplish this when any debatable question is

---

* In Congress this motion is commonly used to defeat a measure, though it does not prevent a majority from taking it up at any other time. Some societies prohibit a question from being taken up from the table, except by a two-thirds vote. This rule deprives the society of the advantages of the motion "to lay on the table," because it would not be safe to lay a question aside temporarily, if one-third of the assembly were opposed to the measure, as that one-third could prevent it ever being taken from the table. A bare majority should not have the power ; in ordinary societies, to adopt or reject a question, or prevent its consideration, without debate. [See note at end of § 35, on the principles involved in making questions undebatable.]

† These motions are strictly for closing or limiting debate, and may be used by either the friends or enemies of a measure. The enemies of a measure may also close debate by suppressing the question itself, as shown in § 59 (a, c).

‡ Except an "objection to the consideration of the question" [§ 59 (a)]. See note to § 35 for a full discussion of this subject of debate.

before the assembly, it is only necessary for some one to obtain the floor and "call for the previous question;" this call being seconded, the chairman, as it allows of no debate, instantly puts the question thus: "Shall the main question be now put?" If this is carried by a two-thirds vote [§ 39] all debate instantly ceases, excepting that in case the pending measure has been reported from a committee the member reporting it is, as in all other cases, entitled to the floor to close the debate; after which the chairman immediately puts the questions to the assembly, first on the motion to commit, if it is pending; if this is carried, of course the subject goes to the committee; if, however, it fails, the vote is next taken on amendments, and finally on the resolution as amended.

If a motion to postpone, either definitely or indefinitely, or a motion to reconsider, or an appeal is pending, the previous question is exhausted by the vote on the postponement, reconsideration or appeal, and does not cut off debate upon any other motions that may be pending. If the call for the previous question fails—that is, the debate is not cut off—the debate continues the same as if this motion had not been made. The previous question can be called for simply on an amendment; and after the amendment has been acted upon, the main question is again open to debate.*

(b) *An Order Limiting or Closing Debate.* Sometimes, instead of cutting off debate entirely, by ordering the previous question, it is desirable to allow of but very limited debate. In this case a motion is made to limit the time allowed each speaker, or the number of speeches on each side, or to appoint a time at which debate shall close and the question be put. The motion may be made to limit debate on an amendment; in which case the main question would afterwards be open to debate and amendment; or it may be made simply on an amendment of an amendment.

In ordinary societies, where harmony is so important, a two-thirds vote should be required for the adoption of any of the above motions to cut off or limit debate.†

---

* As the Previous Question is so generally misunderstood, it would be well to read also what is said upon this subject in § 20.

† In the House of Representatives these motions require only a majority vote for their adoption. In the Senate, on the contrary, not even two-thirds of the members can force a measure to its passage without allowing debate, the Senate rules not recognizing the above motions.

59. To Suppress the Question. (a) *Objection to the Consideration of a Question.* Sometimes a resolution is introduced that the assembly do not wish to consider at all, because it is profitless, or irrelevant to the objects of the assembly, or for other reasons. The proper course to pursue in such cases is for some one, as soon as it is introduced, to "object to the consideration of the question." This objection not requiring a second, the chairman immediately puts the question: "Will the assembly consider this question?" If decided in the negative by a two-thirds vote, the question is immediately dismissed, and cannot be again introduced during that session. This objection must be made when the question is first introduced, before it has been debated, and it can be made when another member has the floor.

(b) *Postpone Indefinitely.* After the question has been debated, the only proper way to suppress it for the session is to vote it down, or to postpone it indefinitely, both of which have the same effect. If the motion to indefinitely postpone is lost, there is still an opportunity for defeating the resolution. It cannot be made while any motion except the original or main question is pending, but it can be made after an amendment has been acted upon, and the main question, as amended, is before the assembly. It opens the merits of the main question to debate to as great an extent as if the main question were before the assembly, and therefore it is necessary also to move the previous question in order to cut off debate and bring the assembly to an immediate vote, just the same as if the question were on the adoption of the resolution.

(c) *Lay on the Table.** If there is no possibility during the remainder of the session of obtaining a majority vote for taking up the question, then the quickest way of suppressing it is to move "to lay the question on the table;" which, allowing of no debate, enables the majority to instantly lay the question on the table, from which it cannot be taken without their consent.

From its high rank [see p. 14] and undebatable character, this motion is very commonly used to suppress a question, but, as shown in § 57 (b), its effect is merely to lay the question aside till the assembly choose

---

* The use of this motion to suppress a question is common, but, as shown in note at close of § 39, a question should not be suppressed and debate prevented by less than a two-thirds vote. See note at close of § 19.

to consider it, and it only suppresses the question so long as there is a majority opposed to its consideration.

60. To Consider a Question a Second Time. *Reconsider.* When a question has been once adopted, rejected, or suppressed it cannot be again considered during that session [§ 42], except by a motion to "reconsider the vote" on that question. This motion can only be made by one who voted* on the prevailing side, and on the day the vote was taken which it is proposed to reconsider, or on the next succeeding day. It can be made and entered on the minutes in the midst of debate, even when another member has the floor, but cannot be considered until there is no question before the assembly, when, if called up, it takes precedence of every motion except to adjourn and to fix the time to which the assembly shall adjourn.

A motion to reconsider a vote on a debatable question, opens to debate the entire merits of the original motion. If the question to be reconsidered is undebatable, then the reconsideration is undebatable.

If the motion to reconsider is carried, the chairman announces that the question now recurs on the adoption of the question the vote on which has been just reconsidered; the original question is now in exactly the same condition that it was in before the first vote was taken on its adoption, and must be disposed of by vote.

When a motion to reconsider is entered on the minutes, it need not be called up by the mover till the next meeting, on a succeeding day.† If he fails to call it up then, any one else can do so. But should there be no succeeding meeting, either adjourned or regular, within a month, then the effect of the motion to reconsider terminates with the adjournment of the meeting at which it was made, and any one can call it up at that meeting.

In general no motion (except to adjourn) that has been once acted upon can again be considered during the same session, except by a motion to reconsider.

---

* In Congress, if the yeas and nays were not taken on the vote, any one can move the reconsideration. The yeas and nays are, however, ordered on all important votes in Congress, which is not the case in ordinary societies.

† If the assembly has not adopted these or similar rules, this paragraph would not apply; but this motion to reconsider would, like any other motion, fall to the ground if not acted upon before the close of the session at which the original vote was adopted.

[The motion to adjourn can be renewed if there has been progress in business or debate, and it cannot be reconsidered.] But this rule does not prevent the renewal of any of the motions mentioned in § 7, provided the question before the assembly has in any way changed; for in this case, while the motions are nominally the same, they are in fact different.*

61. Order and Rules. (*a*) *Orders of the Day.* Sometimes an assembly decides that certain questions shall be considered at a particular time, and when that time arrives those questions constitute what is termed the "orders of the day;" and if any member "calls for the orders of the day," as it requires no second, the chairman immediately puts the question thus: "Will the assembly now proceed to the orders of the day?" If carried, the subject under consideration is laid aside, and the questions appointed for that time are taken up in their order. When the time arrives the chairman may state that fact, and put the above question without waiting for a motion; or, he can announce the orders of the day without taking any vote, if no one objects. If the motion fails, the call for the orders of the day cannot be renewed until the subject then before the assembly is disposed of.†

(*b*) *Special Order.* If a subject is of such importance that it is desired to consider it at a special time, in preference to the orders of the day and established order of business, then a motion should be made to make the question a "special order" for that particular time. This motion requires a two-thirds vote for its adoption, because it is really a suspension of the rules, and it is in order whenever a motion to suspend the rules is in order. If a subject is a special order for a particular day, then on that day it supersedes all business except the reading of the minutes. A special order can be postponed by a majority vote. If two special orders are made for the same day, the one first made takes precedence.

---

*Thus to move to postpone a resolution is a different question from moving to postpone it after it has been amended. A motion to suspend the rules for a certain purpose cannot be renewed at the same meeting, but can be at an adjourned meeting. A call for the orders of the day, that has been negatived, cannot be renewed while the question then before the assembly is still under consideration. [See § 27 for many peculiarities of this motion, and § 25 for the motion to Rescind.]

† See § 13 for a fuller explanation.

(c) *Suspension of the Rules.* It is necessary for every assembly, if discussion is allowed, to have rules to prevent its time being wasted, and to enable it to accomplish the object for which the assembly was organized; and yet at times their best interests are subserved by suspending their rules temporarily. In order to do this some one makes a motion "to suspend the rules that interfere with," etc., stating the object of the suspension. If this motion is carried by a two-thirds vote, then the particular thing for which the rules were suspended can be done. By "general consent," that is, if no one objects, the rules relating to the transaction of business can at any time be ignored without the formality of a motion.

(d) *Questions of Order.* It is the duty of the chairman to enforce the rules and preserve order, and when any member notices a breach of order he can call for the enforcement of the rules. In such cases, when he rises he usually says: "Mr. Chairman, I rise to a point of order." The chairman then directs the speaker to take his seat, and, having heard the point of order, decides the question and permits the first speaker to resume his speech, directing him to abstain from any conduct that was decided to be out of order. When a speaker has transgressed the rules of decorum he cannot continue his speech if any one objects, unless permission is granted him by a vote of the assembly. Instead of the above method, when a member uses improper language, some one says: "I call the gentleman to order," when the chairman decides as before whether the language is disorderly.

(e) *Appeal.* While on all questions of order, and of interpretation of the rules, and of priority of business, it is the duty of the chairman to first decide the question, it is the privilege of any member to "appeal from the decision." If the appeal is seconded, the chairman states his decision, and that it has been appealed from, and then states the question thus: "Shall the decision of the chair stand as the judgment of the assembly [or society, convention, etc.]?"

The chairman can then, without leaving the chair, state the reasons for his decision, after which it is open to debate (no member speaking more than once), excepting in the following cases, when it is undebatable: (1) When it relates to transgressions of the rules of speaking, or to some indecorum, or to the priority of business, and (2) when the previous question was pending at the time the question of order was raised. After the vote is taken, the chairman states that the decision of he chair is sustained, or reversed, as the case may be.

62. Miscellaneous. (a) *Reading of Papers* and (b) *Withdrawal of a Motion.* If a speaker wishes to read a paper, or a member to withdraw his motion after it has been stated by the chair, it is necessary, if any one objects, to make a motion to grant the permission.

(c) *Questions of Privilege.* Should any disturbance occur during the meeting, or anything affecting the rights of the assembly, or any of the members, any member may "rise to a question of privilege," and state the matter, which the chairman decides to be, or not to be, a matter of privilege.* (From the chairman's decision of course an appeal can be taken.) If the question is one of privilege, it supersedes, for the time being, the business before the assembly; its consideration can be postponed to another time, or the previous question can be ordered on it so as to stop debate, or it can be laid on the table, or referred to a committee to examine and report upon it. As soon as the question of privilege is in some way disposed of, the debate which was interrupted is resumed.

63. To Close the Meeting. (a) *Fix the Time to which to Adjourn.*

If it is desired to have an adjourned meeting of the assembly, it is best some time before its close to move, "That when this assembly adjourns, it adjourns to meet at such a time," specifying the time. This motion can be amended by altering the time, but if made when another question is before the assembly, neither the motion nor the amendment can be debated. If made when no other business is before the assembly, it stands as any other main question, and can be debated. This motion can be made even while the assembly is voting on the motion to adjourn, but not when another member has the floor.

(b) *Adjourn.* In order to prevent an assembly from being kept in session an unreasonably long time, it is

---

* A personal explanation is not a matter of privilege. It can be made only by leave of the assembly implied or expressed.

necessary to have a rule limiting the time that the floor can be occupied by any one member at one time.* When it is desired to close the meeting, unless the member who has the floor will yield it, the only resource is to wait till his time expires, and then a member who gets the floor should move "to adjourn." The motion being seconded, the chairman instantly puts the question, as it allows of no amendment or debate; and if decided in the affirmative he says, "The motion is carried; this assembly stands adjourned." If the assembly is one that will have no other meeting, instead of "adjourned," he says, "adjourned without day," or "*sine die.*" If previously it had been decided when they adjourned to adjourn to a particular time, then he states that the assembly stands adjourned to that time. If the motion to adjourn is qualified by specifying the time, as "to adjourn to to-morrow evening," it cannot be made when any other question is before the assembly; like any other main motion, it can then be amended and debated.†

Art. XIII. Miscellaneous

64. Debate. All remarks must be addressed to the chairman and confined to the question before the assembly, avoiding all personalities and reflections upon any one's motives. It is usual for permanent assemblies to adopt rules limiting the number of times any one can speak to the same question, and the time allowed for each speech,‡ as otherwise one member, while he could speak only once to the same question, might defeat a measure by prolonging his speech, and declining to yield the floor except for a motion to adjourn. In ordinary assemblies two speeches should be allowed each member (except upon an appeal), and these rules also limit the time for each speech to ten minutes. A member can be permitted by a two-thirds vote to speak oftener or longer whenever it is desired, and the motion granting such permission cannot be debated. However, if greater freedom is wanted, it is only necessary to

---

* Ten minutes is allowed by these rules.

† See § 11 for effect of an adjournment upon unfinished business.

‡ In Congress, the House of Representatives allows from each member only one speech of one hour's length; the Senate allows two speeches without limit as to length.

consider the question informally, or if the assembly is large, to go into committee of the whole.* If, on the other hand, it is desired to limit the debate more, or close it altogether, it can be done by a two-thirds vote, as shown in § 58 (b).

65. Forms of Stating and Putting Questions. Whenever a motion has been made and seconded, it is the duty of the chairman, if the motion is in order, to state the question, so that the assembly may know what question is before them. The seconding of a motion is required to prevent the introduction of a question when only one member is in favor of it, and consequently but little attention is paid to it in mere routine motions, or when it is evident that many are in favor of the motion; in such cases the chairman assumes that the motion is seconded.

Often in routine work the chairman puts the question without waiting for even a motion,† as few persons like to make such formal motions, and much time would be wasted by waiting for them (but the chairman can only do this as long as no one objects). The following motions, however, do not have to be seconded: (a) a call for the orders of the day; (b) a call to order, or the raising of any question of order; and (c) an objection to the consideration of a question.

One of the commonest forms of stating a question is to say that, "It is moved and seconded that," and then give the motion; or, in case of resolutions, it might be stated in this way (after they have been read): "The question is on the adoption of the resolutions just read."

In some cases, in order to state the question clearly, the chairman should do much more than merely repeat the motion, and say that the question is on its adoption. In the case of an appeal, he should state the decision of the chair (and, if he thinks proper, the reasons for it), and that the decision has been appealed from; he then says, "The question is, shall the decision of the

---

* See §§ 32, 33.

† A presiding officer can frequently expedite business by not waiting for a motion or even taking a vote on a question of routine. In such a case he announces that if there is no objection such will be considered the action of the assembly. For example, when the treasurer's report is read he can say, "If there is no objection the report will be referred to an auditing committee, consisting of Messrs. A. and B."—adding after a moment's pause, "It is so referred."

chair stand as the judgment of the assembly?"* In stating the question on an amendment, the chairman should read (1) the passage to be amended; (2) the words to be struck out, if any; (3) the words to be inserted, if any; and (4) the whole passage as it will stand if the amendment is adopted; he then states the question in a form similar to this: "The question is, shall the word *censure* be inserted in the resolution in the place of the word *thanks?*" As soon as a vote is taken, he should immediately state the question then before the assembly, if there be any. Thus, if an amendment has been voted on, the chairman announces the result, and then says: "The question now recurs on the resolution," or, "on the resolution as amended," as the case may be. So, if an amendment is reconsidered, the chairman should announce the result of the vote and state the question before the assembly in a form similar to this: "The motion is carried—the vote on the amendment is reconsidered; the question recurs on the adoption of the amendment."**

After stating the question on a motion that can be debated or amended, the chairman, unless some one immediately rises, asks: "Are you ready for the question?"† When the chairman thinks the debate is closed, he again inquires: "Are you ready for the question?" If no one rises, he once more states the question as already described, and puts it to vote.

One of the commonest forms of putting the question (after it has been stated) is this: "As many as are in favor of the motion will say *aye;* those opposed will say *no.*" Another one is as follows: "Those in favor of the motion will hold up the right hand; those opposed will manifest it by the same sign."‡

---

* In putting the question to vote after stating it, he should add, "As many as are in favor of sustaining the decision of the chair, say *aye,* as many are opposed say *no.*" If the ayes have it he should then say, "The ayes have it, and the decision of the chair stands as the judgment of the assembly," or, "the decision of the chair is sustained."

** See § 31 for the method of acting on reports of committees and on a paper containing several paragraphs.

† The question, in some societies, is more usually: "Are there any remarks?" or, "Are there any further remarks?"

‡ See §§ 38, 46-48, 54 for examples of various ways of stating and putting questions, and page 10 for peculiar forms.

PART III

MISCELLANEOUS

66. The Right of Deliberative Assemblies to Punish their Members.

A deliberative assembly has the inherent right to make and enforce its own laws and punish an offender—the extreme penalty, however, being expulsion from its own body. When expelled, if the assembly is a permanent society, it has a right, for its own protection, to give public notice that the person has ceased to be a member of that society.

But it has no right to go beyond what is necessary for self-protection and publish the charges against the member. In a case where a member of a society was expelled, and an officer of the society published, by their order, a statement of the grave charges upon which he had been found guilty, the expelled member recovered damages from the officer in a suit for libel, the court holding that the truth of the charges did not affect the case.

67. Right of an Assembly to Eject any one from its Place of Meeting.

Every deliberative assembly has the right to decide who may be present during its session; and when the assembly, either by a rule or by a vote, decides that a certain person shall not remain in the room, it is the duty of the chairman to enforce the rule or order, using whatever force is necessary to eject the party.

The chairman can detail members to remove the person, without calling upon the police. If, however, in enforcing the order, any one uses harsher treatment than is necessary to remove the person, the courts have held that he, and he alone, is liable to prosecution, just the same as a policeman would be under similar circumstances. However badly the man may be abused while being removed from the room, neither the chairman nor the society are liable for damages, as, in ordering his removal, they did not exceed their legal rights.

68. Rights of Ecclesiastical Tribunals.

Many of our deliberative assemblies are ecclesiastical bodies, and it is important to know how much respect will be paid to their decisions by the civil courts.

A church became divided, and each party claimed to be the church, and therefore entitled to the church property. The case was taken into the civil courts, and finally, on appeal, to the U. S. Supreme Court, which held the case under advisement for one year, and then reversed the decision of the State Court, because it conflicted with the decision of the highest ecclesiastical court that had acted upon the case. The Supreme Court, in rendering its decision, laid down the broad principle that, when a local church is but a part of a large and more general organization or denomination, the court will accept the decision of the highest ecclesiastical tribunal to which the case has been carried within that general church organization as final, and will not inquire into the justice or injustice of its decree as between the parties before it. The officers, the ministers, the members, or the church body, which the highest judiciary of the denomination recognizes, the court will recognize. Whom that body expels or cuts off, the court will hold to be no longer members of that church.

69. Trial of Members of Societies.

Every deliberative assembly, having the right to purify its own body, must therefore have the right to investigate the character of its members. It can require any of them to testify in the case, under pain of expulsion if they refuse.

When the charge is against the member's character, it is usually referred to a committee of investigation or discipline, or to some standing committee, to report upon. Some societies have standing committees, whose duty it is to report cases for discipline whenever any are known to them.

In either case the committee investigate the matter and report to the society. This report need not go into details, but should contain their recommendations as to what action the society should take, and should usually close with resolutions covering the case, so that there is no need for any one to offer any additional resolutions upon it. The ordinary resolutions, where the member is recommended to be expelled, are (1) to fix the time to which the society shall adjourn; and (2) to instruct the clerk to cite the member to appear before the society at this adjourned meeting to show cause why he should not be expelled, upon the following charges which should then be given.

After charges are preferred against a member, and the assembly has ordered that he be cited to appear for trial, he is theoretically under arrest, and is deprived of all the rights of membership until his case is disposed of. Without his consent no member should be tried at the same meeting at which the charges are preferred, excepting when the charges relate to something done in that meeting.

The clerk should send the accused a written notice to appear before the society at the time appointed, and should at the same time furnish him with a copy of the charges. A failure to obey the summons is generally cause enough for summary expulsion.

At the appointed meeting what may be called the trial takes place. Frequently the only evidence required against the member is the report of the committee. After it has been read and any additional evidence offered that the committee may see fit to introduce, the accused should be allowed to make an explanation and introduce witnesses, if he so desires. Either party should be allowed to cross-examine the other's witnesses and introduce rebutting testimony. When the evidence is all in, the accused should retire from the room, and the society deliberate upon the question, and finally act by a vote upon the question of expulsion, or other punishment proposed. No member should be expelled by less than a two-thirds* vote—a quorum voting.

In acting upon the case, it must be borne in mind that there is a vast distinction between the evidence necessary to convict in a civil court and that required to convict in an ordinary society or ecclesiastical body. A notorious pickpocket could not even be arrested, much less convicted by a civil court, simply on the

---

* The U.S. Constitution [Art. 1, Sec. 5] provides that each house of Congress may, "with the concurrence of two-thirds, expel a member."

ground of being commonly known as a pickpocket; while such evidence would convict and expel him from any ordinary society.

The moral conviction of the truth of the charge is all that is necessary, in an ecclesiastical or other deliberative body, to find the accused guilty of the charges.

If the trial is liable to be long and troublesome, or of a very delicate nature, the member is frequently cited to appear before a committee, instead of the society, for trial. In this case the committee report to the society the result of their trial of the case, with resolutions covering the punishment which they recommend the society to adopt. When the committee's report is read, the accused should be permitted to make his statement of the case, the committee being allowed to reply. The accused then retires from the room, and the society acts upon the resolutions submitted by the committee. The members of the committee should vote upon the case the same as other members.

If the accused wishes counsel at his trial, it is usual to allow it, provided the counsel is a member of the society in good standing. Should the counsel be guilty of improper conduct during the trial, the society can refuse to hear him, and can also punish him.

70. Call of the House.

The object of a call of the house is to compel the attendance of absent members, and is allowable only in assemblies that have the power to compel the attendance of absentees. It is usual to provide that when no quorum is present, a small number [one-fifth of the members elect in Congress*] can order a call of the house. To prevent this privilege from being used improperly, it is well to provide that when the call is made the members cannot adjourn or dispense with further proceedings in the call until a quorum is ob-

---

* In the early history of our Congress a call of the house required a day's notice, and in the English Parliament it is usual to order that the call shall be made on a certain day in the future, usually not over ten days afterwards, though it has been as long as six weeks afterwards. The object of this is to give notice so that all the members may be present on that day, when important business is to come before the house. In Congress a call of the house is only used now when no quorum is present, and as soon as a quorum appears it is usual to dispense with further proceedings in the call, and this is in order at any stage of the proceedings. In some of our legislative bodies proceedings in the call cannot be dispensed with except a majority of the members elect vote in favor of so doing. In Congress it is customary afterwards to remit the fees that have been assessed.

tained. A rule like the following would answer for city councils and other similar bodies that have the power to enforce attendance:

Rule. When no quorum is present, members may order a call of the house and compel the attendance of absent members. After the call is ordered, a motion to adjourn, or to dispense with further proceedings in the call, cannot be entertained until a quorum is present, or until the sergeant-at-arms reports that in his opinion no quorum can be obtained on that day.

If no quorum is present a call of the house takes precedence of everything, even reading the minutes, except the motion to adjourn, and only requires in its favor the number specified in the rule. If a quorum is present a call should rank with questions of privilege [§ 12], requiring a majority vote for its adoption, and if rejected it should not be renewed, while a quorum is present, at that meeting [see first note to §42]. After a call is ordered, until further proceedings in the call are dispensed with, no motion is in order except to adjourn and a motion relating to the call, so that a recess could not be taken by unanimous consent. An adjournment puts an end to all proceedings in the call, except that the assembly before adjournment, if a quorum is present, can order such members as are already arrested to make their excuses at an adjourned meeting.

Proceedings in a Call of the House. When the call is ordered the clerk calls the roll of members alphabetically, noting the absentees; he then calls over again the names of absentees, when excuses* can be made; after this the doors are locked, no one being permitted to leave, and an order similar in form to the following is adopted: "That the Sergeant-at-Arms take into custody, and bring to the bar of the House, such of its members as are absent without the leave of the House." A warrant signed by the presiding officer and attested by the clerk, with a list of absentees attached, is then given to the sergeant-at-arms,† who immediately proceeds to

---

* It is usual in Congress to excuse those who have "paired off," that is, two members on opposite sides of the pending question who have agreed that both will stay away. In order to "pair off," the absence of both parties must not affect the result, which would rarely be the case in municipal bodies like those under consideration.

† "It shall be the duty of the Sergeant-at-Arms to attend the House during its sittings; to aid in the enforcement of order, under the direction of the Speaker; to execute the commands of the House from time to time; together with all such process, issued by authority thereof, as shall be

arrest the absentees. When he appears with members under arrest, he proceeds to the chairman's desk (being announced by the doorkeeper in large bodies), followed by the arrested members, and makes his return. The chairman arraigns each member separately, and asks what excuse he has to offer for being absent from the sittings of the assembly without its leave. The member states his excuse, and a motion is made that he be discharged from custody and admitted to his seat either without payment of fees or after paying the fees. Until a member has paid the fees assessed against him he cannot vote or be recognized by the chair for any purpose.

---

directed to him by the Speaker." (Rule 22 H.R.) The words "Sergeant-at-Arms" can be replaced in the order by "Chief of Police," or whatever officer is to serve the process.

GUIDE AND COMMENTARY

by

Rachel Vixman

CONTENTS

PART ONE: THE RULES—WHAT THEY MEAN AND WHAT THEY DO

Chapter I
Why Parliamentary Procedure?   130
   Basic Organization Principles   130

Chapter II
What Is the Primary Rule?   131
   Only One Principal or Main Motion at a time   131

Chapter III
Why Other Motions Are Introduced—Their Rank and Order of Procedure   132
   Privileged Motions   132
   Incidental Motions   133
   Subsidiary Motions   135
   To Lay on the Table   137
   More on Amendments   137
   Substitute Motion   138
   Filling Blanks   139

Chapter IV
Miscellaneous and Unclassified Motions   139
   Take from the Table   140
   Reconsider   140
   Reconsider and Enter on the Minutes   140
   Rescind   141
   Renewal   141
   Ratify   141
   Dilatory and Frivolous Motions   141

Chapter V
By Way of Emphasis   141
   Motions That Can Interrupt a Speaker   141

    Motions That Cannot Interrupt a Speaker
      Without His Consent but May
      Interrupt the Proceedings   141
    Motions That Do Not Require a Second   142
    Motions That Cannot Be Amended   142
    Motions That Cannot Be Debated   143
    Motions Requiring a Two-thirds Vote   143
    Motions That Cannot Be Reconsidered   144
    Affirmative Votes That Cannot Be
      Reconsidered   144
    Negative Votes That Cannot Be
      Reconsidered   145
    Motions Classified According to Their
      Objectives   145

Chapter VI
Voting Methods   145

Chapter VII
Know Your Constitution and By-laws   146
    Standing Rules   147

Chapter VIII
Questions and Answers   147

Chapter IX
The Parliamentarian   150

Chapter X
Definition of Parliamentary Terms   152

PART TWO: ORGANIZATION STRUCTURE AND ACCEPTED PROCEDURES

Chapter XI
The Structure   155
    Board of Directors or Trustees   155
    Executive Committee   156
    Standing Committees   156
    Special Committees   157
    Committee of the Whole   158
    Informal Consideration   158

Chapter XII
Officers and Members and Their Respective Duties   158
    President   158
    Vice-President   160

CONTENTS

Recording Secretary 160
Corresponding Secretary 160
Treasurer 160
Assistant Treasurer or Financial Secretary 161
Duties and Rights of Members 161

Chapter XIII
The Meeting Will Come to Order 162
An Example 162
Standard Agenda for Regular Meetings ... 164
Agenda for Special Meeting 165
Suggested Agenda for Annual Meetings ... 165

Chapter XIV
Minutes 166

Chapter XV
Parliamentary Don'ts 167
Don'ts for the Presiding Officer 167
Don'ts for Members 167

Chapter XVI
Speakers Are Human 168

Chapter XVII
Nominations and Elections 169
Nominations 169
Elections 172
Sample Ballot 173

Chapter XVIII
Conventions—Annual, Biennial, or Triennial— of National Federated Bodies with Local Chapters 174

Chapter XIX
Some Useful Miscellaneous Information . 177
Pointers for the President 177
Relationships 178
Social Functions—Guest Seating
and Protocol 179
General 180

Bibliography 182

Diagram of Parliamentary Motions in Order of Precedence 183

Index 185

PART ONE

The Rules—What They Mean and What They Do

Chapter I
WHY PARLIAMENTARY PROCEDURE?

Basic Organization Principles

There is a great need for more democratic policies on organization, communal and national levels.

Since millions of men and women are banded together in hundreds of thousands of organizations—athletic, business, civic, cooperative, cultural, educational, ethnic, fraternal, labor, philanthropic, political, professional, recreational, religious, scientific, social, etc., etc.—the faithful observance of democratic principles would become a major and impressive influence in shaping a stronger American democracy.

Through the ages, parliamentary law has been introduced as organization principles—rules of conduct. It is based on freedom of speech, respect for the dignity of man, equality and justice for all, the principle of majority rule, the right of the minority to be heard, and the duty to abide by the will of the majority.

Robert's Rules of Order has been accepted throughout the United States as the standard authority on parliamentary law and procedure. Hundreds of books have been written to simplify, clarify, and amplify these rules—all based on **Robert's Rules of Order**, rarely changing or superseding this approved work.

There seems to be the mistaken notion that only presidents or aspiring presidents need a knowledge of these rules. It is the member who can change the whole course of the meeting if he has acquired a knowledge of the fundamental laws and procedures. He is then in a position to make a most effective contribution to the group needs; also, he can be on guard to protect the organization when parliamentary law is misused or abused.

General Robert said that if there were no rules or established customs to guide an assembly of persons, and if each could talk on any subject as long and as many times as he pleased, and if all could talk at the same time, it would be impossible in most cases to ascertain their deliberate judgment on any particular matter. Experience has shown the necessity for rules, for a presiding officer to enforce them and to preserve order, and for a recording secretary to keep a record of the business transacted by the assembly.

Chapter II
WHAT IS THE PRIMARY RULE?

Only One Principal or Main Motion at a Time

All business is brought before the meeting by a motion or resolution, a report of a committee or a communication. The terms *motion* and *question* are synonymous; when first stated, it is a *motion,* and when repeated by the chairman, it is referred to as a *question.*

Only one such proposal can be considered at a time. It must be made by a member and seconded by another member. The maker of a motion must get the floor by rising, addressing the presiding officer and obtaining recognition. The motion should be worded in the affirmative whenever possible.

The presiding officer restates the motion and asks, "Are there any remarks?" This opens debate on the question. The maker of the motion is entitled to speak first on the motion. All remarks must be addressed to the chairman. No one may speak a second time on the same question if another member desires to speak on the subject, but he may speak a second time if one who has not spoken is not seeking recognition. But in formal meetings, if anyone objects, he may not speak more often without permission from the assembly.

Motions and resolutions are the same. A *resolution* usually has a preamble or introduction and is much more descriptive, with several paragraphs, starting with "Whereas", and ending with "Therefore, be it resolved". It is subject with slight variations to the same rules as a motion. It is presented in writing. When a main motion is before the assembly, it must be accepted or rejected or be disposed of in some way, before another subject can be introduced, except for privileged or other motions which will be described in following chapters. When a group is prepared to accept a motion in its given form, nothing more is required but to take the vote and get the result. But more often, this is not the case. The assembly may prefer some other course to an immediate decision on the motion in the form in which it is presented. Therefore, it is debated, and *secondary motions* are introduced, which may more clearly meet the wishes of the group.

These secondary motions must be made after the *main* motion is stated and before the vote is taken. When stating the motion, the chairman should make perfectly clear what it is, and, after the vote is taken, state the result.

Motions must not be in violation of local and Federal laws, the organization's constitution and by-laws, or standing rules.

The business of the meeting cannot be conducted unless a quorum is present; the number should be stated in the by-laws. *See RRO,* p. 85.

The chairman should know the rules—when motions can be made, amended, debated, order of precedence, whether they require a majority or two-thirds vote, etc.

See *Robert's Rules of Order,* from very beginning to p. 31.

Also "General Classification of Motions," pp. 31-32.

Chapter III

WHY OTHER MOTIONS ARE INTRODUCED— THEIR RANK AND ORDER OF PROCEDURE

PRIVILEGED MOTIONS

Privileged motions have nothing to do with the pending question or motion, but are of such urgency and importance that they are allowed to interrupt the consideration of other questions, and take precedence over them. They are undebatable because of their high rank. When privileged motions do not interrupt other business, they are *main motions* and are without privileges. There are only five privileged motions, as follows (arranged in order of precedence):

	Second	Debate	Amend	Majority Vote	2/3 Vote	Reconsider	Interrupt
1) Fix time at which to adjourn. See RRO, pp. 33, 115.	*		*	*		*	
2) Adjourn. See RRO, pp. 33, 115.	*			*			
3) Recess (when privileged). See RRO, p. 34.	*		*	*			
4) Raise question of privilege. See RRO, pp. 35, 115.		Chairman‡					*
5) Call for orders of the day. See RRO, pp. 35, 113.		Chairman‡					*

*Asterisks in the table's columns indicate that the motion is seconded, debated, amended, etc. When the line is blank, the chairman deals with the question. This applies to all tables throughout Part One.

‡Chairman (CH hereafter) deals with this—no vote required.

INCIDENTAL MOTIONS

No Order of Precedence Among Themselves

Incidental motions are those which arise out of a pending question and must be decided before any other business is taken up; or are something connected with the business of the assembly that must be attended to and which requires a temporary interruption. They have no special rank among themselves, but they yield to privileged questions. They are dealt with individually as they arise, but they take precedence over the subsidiary motions. Most of them are undebatable.

Points of order, parliamentary inquiries, and requests for information do not require action by the assembly. The presiding officer takes care of these unless they need to be referred to the group for consideration.

The incidental motions are as follows (all of equal rank):

	Second	Debate	Amend	Majority Vote	2/3 Vote	Reconsider	Interrupt
Point of order. RRO, pp. 38, 113.			CH				*
Appeal from decision of chair. RRO, pp. 38, 114, 117.	*	*1		*		*	*
Objection to consideration of question. RRO, pp. 39, 111.					*	*2	*
Request to read papers. RRO, pp. 39, 115.	*			*		*2	
Division of a question. RRO, pp. 30, 49, 108.	*		*	*			*
To withdraw a motion. RRO, pp. 40, 115.		CH				*2	
To suspend the rules. RRO, pp. 40, 114.	*				*		
Methods of voting. RRO, pp. 71, 106, 117.	*		*	*			
Division of assembly. RRO, p. 72.			CH				
Close nominations or polls[3]. RRO, p. 73.	*		*		*		
Reopen nominations or polls[3]. RRO, p. 73.	*		*	*		*2	
Consideration by paragraph or seriatim. RRO, pp. 62, 95.	*	*	*	*4		*2	*
Requests for information. p. 50		CH					*
Parliamentary inquiry.		CH					*
Filling blanks. RRO, p. 50.				*		*2	
Question of quorum present. RRO, p. 85.		CH					*

[1] There are one or more exceptions. See RRO, pp. 38, 114.

[2] The motion can be reconsidered only if the *prevailing* vote was a negative one.

[3] Chapter XVII deals with "Nominations and Elections."

[4] If the paragraphs refer to by-laws, they require a two-thirds vote.

SUBSIDIARY MOTIONS

The *subsidiary motions* are the most frequently used motions in parliamentary procedure. They are made while a main motion is pending, for the purpose of assisting or modifying it or to delay action or otherwise dispose of the main motion. The subsidiary motion supersedes the main motion for the time being and must be dealt with before action can be taken on the main motion. However, all subsidiary motions must yield to privileged and incidental motions.

There are only seven subsidiary motions, and they rank in the following order:

	Second	Debate	Amend	Majority Vote	2/3 Vote	Reconsider	Interrupt
1) Lay on the table. RRO, pp. 41, 109, 111.	*			*			
2) Previous question—close debate. RRO, pp. 42, 109.	*				*	*1	
3) Limit or extend debate, RRO, pp. 76, 110, 116.	*		*		*	*	
4) Postpone to a certain time. RRO, pp. 47, 108.	*	*	*	*		*	
5) Commit or refer. pp. 47, 108.	*	*	*	*		*	
6) Amend. RRO, Index—Amendment.	*	*	*	*		*	
7) Postpone indefinitely. RRO, pp. 51, 111.	*	*		*		* Only affirmative vote	
Main Motion	*	*	*	*	*	*	

[1] There are several exceptions. RRO, p. 43.

The first, as listed, is of higher rank than every motion listed below it. This means that a motion of higher rank can always be entertained while a motion of lower rank is pending before the house, but a motion of lower rank cannot be entertained if a motion of higher rank is before the body.

Example: If a secondary motion has been made "to commit," which means to "refer to a committee," and another member moves "the previous question" (close debate) which is of a higher rank, the chairman should state, "The motion just proposed is not in order because it is of lower rank than the pending question 'the previous question.'"

The chairman states the motion on "the previous question" when Mr. B. interrupts: "Mister President, I move to lay the motion on the table." It is seconded. (Since this has the highest rank of all proposed, it is entertained.)

Chair: "It is moved and seconded to lay the motion on the table."

Mr. C: "I move the previous question."

Chair: "The motion just proposed is *not in order* because it is of lower rank than the motion to table."

Mr. D: "I move to amend the main motion by adding 'and the class should be limited to fifteen.'" (The main motion before the house was "to have a parliamentary class.")

Chair: "The amendment just proposed is not in order; it is of lower rank than the motion to table."

Mr. E: "Mister President, how many motions are now pending?"

Chair: "Five motions: namely, to refer to a committee, the previous question, to table, an amendment, and the *main* motion 'to have a parliamentary class.'"

Then the Chair (applying the rule that when more than one motion is before the house, the motion having the highest rank must be put to vote first, and if defeated, the next highest, etc.) states: "Those in favor of 'tabling the motion' say 'aye'; those opposed, say 'no'; ... the noes have it—the motion is lost. Those in favor of the previous question, to close debate, will rise; those opposed, please rise. This requires a two-thirds vote. ... The motion is lost. The motion now in order is to refer this motion to a committee. Is there any discussion? Are you ready for the vote? Those in favor say 'aye' ... those opposed say 'no.'" ...

The motion is passed and the main motion is referred to a committee. If the members had preferred to make an immediate decision, they would have defeated the motion to refer and the main motion would be acted upon. There could also have been interruptions with privileged and incidental motions which take precedence. This, of course, is not a usual procedure.

TO LAY ON THE TABLE

To lay on the table is a tricky motion and is often used to suppress a question. It has the highest rank among the subsidiary motions, cannot be debated or amended, and, if seconded, must immediately be put to a vote. Its real intent is to move aside a pending question *temporarily* when consideration must be given to some business of an urgent nature.

After the business has been taken care of, it should be moved "to take from the table" the motion that was laid aside, and seconded. This must be done during the same session or at the very next meeting—otherwise it lapses and the motion is dead.

If a majority vote cannot be secured "to take it from the table," to "lay it on the table" was then a deliberate attempt to suppress the motion.

The "legitimate" motions to use, if one wants to "kill" a motion, are "to postpone indefinitely" or "to object to the consideration of the question."

MORE ON AMENDMENTS

General Robert emphasizes the need to understand the subject of amendments, in his opinion, which, are the most important, and, perhaps, the most difficult part of parliamentary law. Since amendments play such an important part, this will stress some important details.

Amendments are introduced to assist in changing, modifying, or helping to complete a motion in such a way as to make it more acceptable to the assembly. Main motions when first presented are not usually made complete enough in their most essential particulars. Through amendments—in adding, striking out, inserting, or substituting words—these changes make the motion more complete and desirable.

An amendment must be germane to the subject of the motion—directly relating to it, even if taking an opposite point of view. Amendments are seconded, debated, amended, and require a majority vote. They can be reconsidered. Amendments to main motions can be proposed only when nothing of higher rank than the motion "to postpone indefinitely" is pending.

Not more than two amendments to a motion are permitted—it would otherwise become too complicated. The first amendment is called the *primary amendment*—the second, the *secondary amendment*. When the first amendment is made, the vote must be taken on the amendment first, and, if adopted, *the original motion, as amended*, must be stated and discussed, then put to vote. If there are two amendments, the latter amendment (secondary) is voted on first. It must apply to the first amendment and not to the main motion. If adopted, the *first* or *primary amendment as amended* must then be voted on (adopted) and finally the *main motion as amended*. Until the *main motion has been voted on or disposed of*, there is no decision and *no other main motion may be introduced*.

While there cannot be more than two amendments pending at a time, if they are voted down, other amendments may be presented. In RRO, p. 51, this helpful statement appears. "When a member desires to move an amendment that is not in order at the time but affects the pending question, he should state his intention of offering his amendment if the pending amendment is voted down. In this way those who favor his amendment will vote in the negative [on the pending amendment], and if they succeed in killing [the amendment], then the new amendment can be offered."

SUBSTITUTE MOTION

A *substitute motion* should be introduced if amendments become involved or a paragraph requires considerable changes. This will be considered as an amendment of the first degree. It cannot be made when an amendment is pending. The treatment is different than that accorded a regular amendment. The Chair states the substitute motion when proposed and then returns to the pending main motion for debate and one amendment only—but the original main motion is not put to a vote at that time. The subsitute motion is then open to debate and one amendment. The vote is then taken on the substitute motion first (same as with the regular amendment); if the substitute is adopted, the main motion *as substituted* is put to a vote. If substitute amendment is not adopted, the main motion is voted on.

FILLING BLANKS

Filling blanks is an informal motion that provides for amendments to be made differently—not limited to two amendments but permits any number of suggestions or amendments to be made, then voting on each in turn until a majority vote is secured. It saves time in making formal amendments—requires no second, and permits members to call out numbers, dates, nominations, etc. Sometimes, the largest number or the most distant date—sometimes, when more feasible, the lowest number—is voted on first and voted on in turn, until a majority vote is reached.

Example: "Mr. Chairman, I move that we buy some new furniture for the recreation room, at a cost not to exceed blank dollars."

"Seconded."

Chairman: "What sum shall be inserted to fill the blank?"

Members: "$1,000." "$700." "$500." "$250." (Any member may call out in any order.)

When no further suggestions are made, the chairman proceeds to take a vote, starting with the largest sum, until a satisfactory sum receives a majority vote. This can be applied with dates, nominations, etc. When applied to nominations, the vote should be taken on names in the order called out. Though permitted, it is not wise to deal with nominations in this form, for the first nominee may secure a *majority vote* (members do not wish to oppose a candidate openly) and no other names can then be submitted.

Chapter IV

MISCELLANEOUS AND UNCLASSIFIED MOTIONS

There are a few main motions, not classified, which are very much in use in an effort to take up a question again, or to change or undo an action that has been taken. In certain situations, some members believe there has been too small an attendance at the meeting or that it has been an unrepresentative one; therefore, they desire a new ruling on the subject. These motions have *no* order of precedence. They are as follows:

	Second	Debate	Amend	Majority Vote	⅔ Vote	Reconsider	Interrupt
Take from table. RRO, pp. 41, 109.	*			*			
Reconsider. RRO, pp. 53, 112.	*	*1		*			*
Reconsider and enter on the minutes. RRO, pp. 28, 53, 112.	*	No further action until next meeting. Must be called up at next meeting					
Rescind (repeal). RRO, p. 52.	*	*	*	with NOTICE *	without notice *	*2	*
Renewal of a motion. RRO, pp. 52, 83, 113.	*	*		*			
Ratify	*	*	*	*		*2	
Dilatory and frivolous motions. RRO, p. 79.				CH			

[1] It is undebatable if the motion to reconsider is undebatable.
[2] Motion can be reconsidered only if *prevailing* vote was a negative one.

TAKE FROM TABLE

See Page 13.

RECONSIDER

The motion to reconsider is made only by one who voted on the prevailing side. If a member considers the action taken not in the best interest of the organization and would wish the group to reconsider it, he is advised to change his *minority* vote to that of the majority before the vote is taken, to be on the prevailing side. Anyone can second the motion to reconsider.

This motion can be made *only on the day the vote was taken* (or the day after, at a conference or convention that lasts several days).

If the motion is carried, the original motion is again open to discussion and vote. No question can be twice reconsidered unless it was materially amended after its first reconsideration.

RECONSIDER AND ENTER ON THE MINUTES

The motion to reconsider and enter on the minutes is a *protective measure to stop any action from being taken* if there is no possibility of a change in the vote. It serves notice that the action should be taken up at the *next* meeting. A number of parliamentarians have taken issue on this motion, claiming it would permit a few to obstruct action, but General Robert clearly states that this action will prevent a temporary majority, due to a small quorum present, to take action that may be detrimental to the best interests of the organization.

This motion *outranks the motion to reconsider* and can be made immediately after the other, providing a vote has not yet been taken on it. It should then be taken up at the *very next meeting*, subject to same rules as reconsideration. (Requires a Second.)

RESCIND

The motion to rescind requires a two-thirds vote if notice of the motion to be proposed has not been given at the preceding meeting or in the call of the meeting. A motion to rescind is not in order if action has already been taken which cannot be undone.

RENEWAL

See *RRO* pp. 52, 83, 113.

RATIFY

An emergency measure may sometimes be taken by an officer or officers or at a meeting without a quorum, which requires ratification or approval at a duly constituted meeting.

DILATORY AND FRIVOLOUS MOTIONS

Dilatory and frivolous motions are not to be entertained and should be declared out of order.

Chapter V

BY WAY OF EMPHASIS

MOTIONS THAT CAN INTERRUPT A SPEAKER

A call for the orders of the day
A point of order
A question of privilege
A question of quorum

MOTIONS THAT CANNOT INTERRUPT A SPEAKER WITHOUT HIS CONSENT BUT MAY INTERRUPT THE PROCEEDINGS

Appeal from decision of Chair
Giving notice of reconsideration or repeal

Objection to consideration of a question
Parliamentary inquiry
Point of information
Request that the question be divided

MOTIONS THAT DO NOT REQUIRE A SECOND

Call for the division of the assembly (recount of vote)
Call for the division of the question under certain circumstances
Call up motion to reconsider
Call for the orders of the day
Committee and board recommendations—motions
Filling blanks
Inquiries of any kind
Leave to withdraw a motion (if not stated by the Chair)
Nominations
Objection to the consideration of the question
Parliamentary inquiry
Point of information
Point of order
Question of privilege

MOTIONS THAT CANNOT BE AMENDED

Adjourn (except when qualified or when made with no provision for future meeting)
Amend an amendment
Appeal
Call for the orders of the day
Call for a division of the assembly (voting)
Fill a blank
Grant leave to withdraw a motion
Lay on the table
Leave to read papers
Nomination
Object to consideration of a question
Postpone indefinitely
Previous question
Question of order
Question of privilege
Reconsider and call up question to reconsider
Request of any kind
Take from the table
Take up a question out of its proper order
(Every original main motion and resolution may be amended.)

MOTIONS THAT CANNOT BE DEBATED

Adjourn
Amend an undebatable motion
Appeal (under certain circumstances; see RRO, pp. 37, 114)
Call for the orders of the day
Call up motion to reconsider
Dispense with the reading of the minutes
Fix the time to which to adjourn (when privileged)
Lay on the table
Limit or extend debate
Objection to the consideration of a question
Other incidental motions, which include the following:
  Close or reopen nomination
  Close or reopen the polls
  Division of assembly
  Division of a question
  Filling a blank
  Point of order, information, inquiry
  Question of quorum present
  Voting, motions relating to methods of
  Withdraw a motion
Previous question (close debate)
Raise a question of privilege
Reconsider an undebatable motion
Suspension of the rules
Take a recess (when privileged)
Take from the table

MOTIONS REQUIRING A TWO-THIRDS VOTE

(Used in all situations when a change of constitution and bylaws is adopted or where some right of the membership is curtailed.)

To amend (annul, repeal, or rescind) any part of constitution, by-laws, etc. previously adopted; also requires previous notice

To amend or rescind a standing rule, order of business, or a resolution, previously adopted, if previous notice was not given

Close nominations or the polls limiting the names to be voted for at an election

Correction of adopted minutes if proposed at a later meeting than the one at which it was originally adopted, unless previous notice of the proposed amendment (correction) has been given

Depose from office (also requires previous notice)

Discharge a committee when previous notice has not been given

Discharge an order of the day prior to the time set

Expel from membership (also requires previous notice and trial)

Extend the time set for adjournment or for taking a recess

To limit or extend debate

To make a special order of business

The previous question (close debate)

Refuse to take up an order of the day

To repeal or rescind that which has been adopted unless previous notice has been given

To suspend the rules

Sustain an objection to the consideration of a question

To take up a question out of its proper order

MOTIONS THAT CANNOT BE RECONSIDERED

Adjourn
Call for the orders of the day
Division of the assembly
Division of the question
Lay on the table
Main motions executed in whole or partially
Nominations, to make or to close
Parliamentary or other inquiry
Raise question of order or privilege
Reconsider
Suspend the rules of order of business
Take a recess
Take from the table

AFFIRMATIVE VOTES THAT CANNOT BE RECONSIDERED

(Such affirmative votes can be reconsidered only if negative side prevails.)

Accept resignation, if member is present or has been notified. Reopen nominations

Adopt, or after adoption, to amend, or repeal, or rescind the constitution, bylaws, or rules of order, or any other rules that require previous notice for their amendment

Elect to membership or office if the member or

officer is present and does not decline, or if absent
has learned of his election in the usual way and
has not declined

Proceed to the orders of the day

NEGATIVE VOTES THAT CANNOT BE RECONSIDERED

The motion to postpone indefinitely cannot be
reconsidered if the negative side prevails

No question can be twice reconsidered unless it
was materially amended after its first reconsideration. A reconsideration requires only a majority
vote, regardless of the vote necessary to adopt the
motion itself

The motion to reconsider cannot be in force after
the next day when proposed

MOTIONS CLASSIFIED ACCORDING TO THEIR OBJECTIVES

See RRO, p. 107

Chapter VI

VOTING METHODS

See RRO. pp. 71, 117

All motions are divided into two classes—debatable
and undebatable. Undebatable motions are put to a
vote immediately, after the chairman states the motion.
Some motions require a majority vote, a number greater than half the votes cast, others a two-thirds vote.
One of the fundamental principles of parliamentary
law requires a two-thirds vote for every motion *that
suppresses a main question without free debate*. Sometimes a vote is unanimous. A plurality vote—the most
votes cast for a candidate—is used only in elections
when authorized by bylaws.

There are many methods of taking the vote. Those
most used are by *voice* (viva voce) *aye* and *no, raising
right hand* or *rising, ballot* (usually authorized in elections), *roll call, general consent*.

If membership is scattered and the bylaws authorize
it, voting is also done by mail on important matters,
such as election of officers and amending bylaws.

Proxy voting is usually promoted by stock corporations, etc., but is not practical for the average group.

On courtesy votes, such as a "vote of thanks to the speaker," the negative vote is not put.

While parliamentary rules permit a chairman to vote on any question when his vote will change the result, it is wiser that a president should avoid showing partisanship on a moot question. He should vote when a ballot is used (usually for elections). His name is called last when a roll call is used.

By general consent or unanimous vote: this ruling is used to avoid the formality of taking the vote when there seems to be no objection to the question. It is used when routine business is conducted and on minor matters. Instead of taking a vote, the chairman says, "If there is no objection," and assumes general consent, unless someone objects. Then a vote must be taken.

In the case of approving the minutes and asking for corrections, no motion is required. The chairman states, "If there is no objection, the minutes stand approved as read [or corrected]."

Chapter VII
KNOW YOUR CONSTITUTION AND BYLAWS
See RRO, pp. 95-98

It is assumed that the groups are already organized and have adopted a constitution and bylaws. Sometimes they are one and the same—if divided, the most important rules are placed in the constitution, those most likely to be changed, in the bylaws. The pages listed above from *Robert's Rules of Order* give the rules for drafting and adopting a constitution, etc.

Once the organization adopts the basic structure and rules by which it is to be guided, these rules must be adhered to, and *supersede* standard parliamentary laws and only *such rules which are not included* are governed by the standard parliamentary authority adopted.

Provision should be made for amendments to the constitution and bylaws. This provision should not be too rigid, since *emergencies* do arise which cannot be foreseen. Usually, amendments are presented at annual meetings and conventions, and require a two-thirds vote of those voting and notice given in advance at a time period listed, or three-fourths vote of those voting if no notice has been given.

General Robert states that if the constitution, bylaws, and rules of order that have been adopted contain no rule for their amendment, they may be amended at any regular business meeting by a vote of the *majority of the entire membership,* or, if the amendment was submitted in writing at the previous regular business meeting, then they may be amended by a *two-thirds vote of those voting*—a quorum being present.

In writing a constitution, it is customary to use *Roman numerals for article* headings but *simple figures for sections.*

National organizations provide their chapters or units with "model" constitutions conforming to national policy, to be filled in with minor details for local needs.

No motion or resolution is in order that conflicts with the constitution and bylaws or standing rules, if any have been adopted.

STANDING RULES
See RRO, p. 98

Chapter VIII
QUESTIONS AND ANSWERS

Q. Do we really need the confusing motion "previous question"?

A. No. Its usual justifiable use could be better served by the simple motion "close debate." General Robert uses this terminology on p. 71.

Q. In a parliamentary study group, X says that the adoption of a motion to "lay on the table" kills the motion tabled. Y says that is does not kill. Who is correct?

A. Laying the question on the table does not kill it, except by virtue of a special rule in some organizations. When an assembly has something before it that claims its attention, it is intended to lay aside a proposition for a short, but indefinite time. It may be taken from the table by a majority vote at any time when no question is pending during this or the next session. If not taken from the table then, it is "killed."

Q. While a motion was under consideration, someone moved, and it was seconded, that it be referred to the house committee. Before the Chair put the motion to a vote, someone moved an amendment to the main motion. The chair moved the motion to amend out of order. Was this ruling correct?

A. Yes. "Referring to a committee" is of higher rank than amending, and while a motion of higher rank is pending, one of the lower rank is not in order.

Q. If a member requests that his vote be recorded in the minutes, should the Chair ask if there is any objection?

A. Yes. If there is no objection, the Chair directs the secretary to make the entry. If objection is made, the Chair puts the question to vote.

Q. The bylaws of a society provide that the executive board shall consist of the officers, department chairmen, and chairmen of standing committees. Elsewhere is a clause empowering the president to appoint the chairmen of standing committees. Is it legal for an appointed chairman to be a member of the board?

A. The constitution and bylaws are the organized law of the society, and as long as they do not conflict with national or state laws, or the vested rights of members, or plain principles of justice, you may place in them any provision the assembly chooses. The method of choosing the chairman of a committee in no way affects the question of his rights and duties.

Q. Is it unconstitutional for a constitution to require payment of dues of its members in advance?

A. No. Nothing in a constitution can be unconstitutional, which means "in violation of the constitution." A society has a perfect right to make such a provision in its constitution.

Q. Are the names of the makers of motions always entered in the minutes?

A. It is well to enter in the minutes the names of the persons offering motions. The names of the seconders need not be entered. But every society has the right to decide what names should be entered in the minutes, and may enter the seconder's name if it so chooses.

Q. What would be the procedure in the event of a nominating committee unable to nominate a president, and, under the bylaws, nominations from the floor are not allowed?

A. Ballot for officers, without nominations, or, if preferred, a nominating ballot could be taken first.

QUESTIONS AND ANSWERS

Q. Is it legal for a nominating committee to present two names for the same office to the voting body?

A. Yes. If the assembly in such case wishes the committee to submit only one name, it can refer the report back to the committee with instructions to that effect. Sometimes, the committee is required to submit two names for each office.

Q. How are committees chosen?

A. If the bylaws do not rule on this, the general procedure is to have the chairman appoint them. The first name mentioned is considered the chairman.

Care should be taken in naming the first. Often the chairman is named or election of a chairman is desired by the committee. If they are standing committees, it often serves the purpose better to allow the chairman of the committee to choose his own members of the committee.

If the committee is to be a special one, it is necessary for the assembly to decide how it is to be named, whether appointed or elected, and how many members it should have. If different methods are suggested, or moved, they are voted on in the following order: ballot; nominations from the floor; nominations by the chair; and lastly, appointments by the Chair, the method that should usually be adopted in large assemblies. It is the usual thing to appoint to the committee the person who made the motion to refer to a committee, when he is specially interested or informed on the subject.

Q. Can there be more than one motion before the house at one time?

A. Yes. There can be only one *main* motion at a time. However, secondary motions can be proposed and entertained while a main motion is pending, such as amending, postponing, referring to a committee, etc., etc. The main motion is of the lowest rank and these other motions (in accordance with their rank) must be disposed of before the main motion.

Q. Should the recording secretary include in the minutes a motion that has been withdrawn?

A. No. When a motion is withdrawn, the effect is the same as if it had never been made.

Q. No minutes are read or reports given of the meetings of the board which are held a week before the general meeting. Is this correct procedure?

A. Minutes of board meetings are not read at general meetings. But most groups that meet monthly limit the power of the board and call for reports and any recommendations it is prepared to make. It is then up for discussion and ratification or otherwise by the general membership.

Q. What is meant by a point of order?

A. A point of order is raised when there is a violation of the rules of order or of the bylaws or when a member is not speaking on the motion before the house. A point of order can interrupt a speaker to ensure orderly procedure.

Q. A large convention is reportedly interrupted so that the stenotypist can get the name of the second to each motion. Are such delays advisable?

A. No. It is not necessary for the stenographic record of the minutes to include the names of seconds, and it is important to avoid unnecessary interruptions.

Q. Are board meetings conducted formally or informally?

A. In large boards, business is transacted the same as in "society" meetings; but in small boards, the same formality is not necessary or usual. The procedure observed is that of committees, which is informal. In a board meeting of not more than a dozen, it is not necessary to rise to make a motion, nor to wait for recognition before speaking, nor is there any limit to the number of speeches. The chairman is much freer in discussing a question.

Chapter IX

THE PARLIAMENTARIAN

Most state and national organizations utilize the services of a professional parliamentarian. They may have in their midst officers and members who are proficient in parliamentary procedure, but they find it preferable to engage the services of a nonmember, whose objectivity and impartiality will not be questioned. A parliamentarian is one who is versed in the rules and procedures of parliamentary law. He is engaged at such meetings to advise the presiding officer on questions of procedure in transacting the business of the assembly legally, efficiently, and impartially. (It would be well to include the need for this service in the bylaws). He is usually chosen by the president, or approved by the board.

The parliamentarian is introduced just before the business session commences. He is assigned a seat near the presiding officer for convenient consultation. The delegates are made aware that a competent parliamentarian is on hand to advise the chairman (he does not make decisions) and, when necessary, *if asked by the chairman or the assembly,* to state the ruling or give his interpretation of it. He gets a copy of the constitution and bylaws, standing rules, program, and general information before the meeting to familiarize himself with their basic rules. It is also helpful for him to meet with the presiding officer in advance, when feasible.

Questions or inquiries intended for the parliamentarian should be addressed to him through the Chair, because the Chair is the presiding officer, who, in turn, gives the answer if he knows it, or gets the answer from the parliamentarian. The parliamentarian does not hesitate to advise the presiding officer when serious errors occur, but the responsibility for the decisions rests with the chairman, who is in control. The parliamentarian's opinion is purely advisory; the house may appeal from the president's decision, when he does not conform to the rules.

A parliamentarian may be asked to give, by telephone or in writing, opinions on parliamentary problems. He gives advice to groups, sometimes is asked to render an opinion directly to an assembly, takes part in workshops, seminars, conferences, caucuses. He may help draft bylaws, resolutions, minutes, etc. He teaches classes in parliamentary law and procedure. He gives lectures on the subject. He should emphasize not only the basic principles of parliamentary law, but also ethical techniques by which one can render effective service.

Chapter X
DEFINITION OF PARLIAMENTARY TERMS

Accept, Adopt, Approve, applied to reports and motions agreed upon—not to be confused with "received."

Adjourn, to bring the meeting to a close.

Agenda, the order of business to be brought up at a meeting.

Amend, to change or modify a motion by striking out, or by adding or by substituting.

Assembly, a group, society, club, sometimes called "the house."

Business, motion, resolution, subject, the proceedings; the agenda.

Bylaws, code of rules or regulations accepted by a society for its own guidance.

Chair, the presiding officer at a meeting.

Clerk, same as secretary.

Commit, to refer to a committee.

Constitution, same as bylaws; sometimes combined, or in two parts. The constitution contains the more basic essentials; the other, procedures.

Debate, to discuss the pros and cons of a motion.

Division of Assembly or the House, calling for a recount of the vote.

Division of a Question, separating a motion and voting on each part separately.

Executive Secretary, a salaried executive, as a general manager under the board and executive committee.

Ex-officio, by virtue of official position, usually of boards and committees.

Fiscal Year, the financial year of an organization.

Floor, Obtain the, when a member is recognized by the Chair, he has the "floor."

Floor, On the, a motion is on the floor when it is being considered by the assembly.

General Consent, unanimous, silent, used in routine matters, if there is no objection, avoiding a formal vote.

Germane, relevant, pertinent to the pending question.

Good of the Order, Good and Welfare, after the business, if there is time, general discussions, constructive criticism, informal suggestions.

PARLIAMENTARY TERMS

House, same as assembly, meeting, etc.

Main Motion, the motion that introduces the business or a proposal to the assembly for action.

Majority, more than half the votes cast.

Minutes, the official record of proceedings at a meeting.

Motion, Main or Principal, See *Main Motion.*

Order of Business, same as agenda—the schedule of business to be considered.

Orders of the Day, program or order of business adopted that should be followed.

Parliamentarian, one skilled in parliamentary procedure; advises the presiding officer concerning questions of parliamentary procedure.

Parliamentary Law, accepted rules for deliberative bodies, mostly derived from the usage of the English Parliament and later from the United States Congress.

Pending and Immediately Pending, the question before the assembly for discussion and action.

Plurality, term used in an election when one candidate has the largest number of votes.

Point of Order, a question concerning a breach of parliamentary rules.

Postpone Indefinitely, a motion to suppress, eliminate, or "kill" the main motion.

Preamble, an introduction or a preface to a resolution.

Precedence, priority in rank.

Prevailing Side, the side having secured the most votes.

Previous Question, a call to close debate and take the vote.

Privilege, Questions of, must not be confused. It refers to rights and privileges of the assembly or any of its members.

Pro Tem, for the time being, temporary.

Putting the Question, placing the motion before the assembly for a vote.

Question, same as motion, when stated by the Chair for a vote.

Quorum, a specified number of members required, according to the bylaws, to hold a legal meeting.

Recess, a motion used to halt the proceedings temporarily.

Refer, see *Commit.*

Seriatim Consideration, consideration of a motion, line by line and paragraph by paragraph.

Sine Die, without a day, indefinitely, final adjournment.

Table a Motion, to put aside the pending question temporarily.

Table, Take from, a motion used to restore a question for consideration again.

Ticket, a slate of candidates for office.

Two-thirds Vote, two-thirds of the vote cast; it should be a rising vote.

Viva Voce, by the voice; usually is the method of voting.

Voting, those actually casting a vote.

Yield, concede to, outranked by, give way to.

PART TWO

Organization Structure and Accepted Procedures

Chapter XI
THE STRUCTURE

BOARD OF DIRECTORS OR TRUSTEES
See RRO, pp. 48, 56, 65, 85, 90, 100, 104, 108

The *board of directors* is a connecting link between the officers and membership and usually plays an important part in larger organizations in developing projects, policies, and personnel to carry out the activities of the organization. The *executive board* or *board of directors*, or *trustees* or *managers* (all the same) are usually elected by the membership at an annual meeting and are given responsibility for transacting the business between meetings. The board usually consists of the officers, chairmen of standing committees, and a few other representative members. General Robert considers the board a standing committee, but most organizations indicate in their constitution and bylaws the assumption of greater responsibilities and supervision. The president may be the chairman of the board, or the bylaws may give the board the privilege of electing its chairman, who may still be the president. The bylaws should be explicit in defining the functions and powers of the board. The board and officers are subordinate to the organization and must abide by constitutional rulings, and also by convention action.

Many organizations, meeting quarterly or annually, give their boards full power to carry on the general administration. But the average volunteer club limits the board, when new policies or projects are considered, to reporting to the general membership for approval and ratification.

The minutes of meetings of the board are not read at the membership meeting, but a report is given by the presiding officer or someone designated to report.

Officers and directors are elected annually or for a longer period as specified in the bylaws. Frequently, directors are elected for a three-year period, and one-third of its members "expires" each year.

In some organizations, the board elects the officers and committees. When a new board is elected, new appointments of standing chairmen may be made, and all unfinished business falls to the ground unless desired.

EXECUTIVE COMMITTEE

Most organizations make provision in their bylaws for an *executive committee,* with a board of directors or without. This committee includes the officers of the organization, and many groups broaden its scope by having the board elect a certain number of others.

This executive committee strengthens the position of the president, and transacts routine business between meetings of the board and acts in emergencies.

In many groups, the president, with the approval of the executive committee, appoints the chairmen of committees, unless otherwise prescribed in the bylaws.

All business transacted by the executive committee is reported to the board at its next meeting.

The executive committee meets at the call of the president or upon written request of any ——— members thereof.

——— members shall constitute a quorum for the transaction of all business.

STANDING COMMITTEES
See RRO, p. 56.

Standing committees are usually committees named in the bylaws to function throughout the year. These committees are given responsibilities to further various departments or projects. The usual standing committees are membership, fund-raising, budget and finance, program, social or hospitality, international affairs, legislation, arts, resolutions, etc., depending on the purpose of the organization.

Committees function in a very informal fashion, observing none of the formal rules.

A vote should be taken on most questions.

The chairman of a committee usually does most of the talking, but should encourage all members to express their opinions. He votes on all questions.

If a chairman is absent, or fails to call a meeting of his committee, any two members may issue the call, but a majority of the committee should be present before any action is taken.

A committee should not involve the organization in any way or incur debts unless given the authority to do so by the organization.

These committees are expected to submit reports, when desired, and at annual meetings. In submitting a report with a recommendation, the chairman of the committee should move its adoption before taking his seat. This does not require a second since it is the proposal of a committee. It should be stated as a motion by the presiding officer, followed by discussion, and the vote taken.

SPECIAL COMMITTEES
See RRO, p. 104

Special committees are appointed or elected at a business meeting following a motion "to commit"—meaning, to refer to a committee—to perform some special task, secure more information, investigate a situation, and bring back a report or a recommendation to the membership meeting.

These are temporary committees which cease to function when they have completed their duties and brought in a report.

When it is intended to give the committee full power without referring it back to a membership meeting, the words "with full power" should be added to the motion to commit—to refer to a committee.

No further action is taken on the motion by the assembly until the committee reports.

Minority vote—when a motion has been referred to a committee and one or more members of the committee differ from the majority point of view, the minority report is an accepted form of democratic procedure. The procedure is as follows:

The report of the special committee (it is not called

a majority report) is given at the meeting when called upon, and the committee chairman, after giving the report, moves its adoption. When seconded, the presiding officer states: "It has been moved and seconded that ———— [stating the motion]. Is there any discussion?"

Minority member immediately moves to substitute a minority report for that of the committee and states the minority report. Seconded.

Chairman: "It has been moved and seconded to substitute the minority report for the report of the committee ———— [restates the minority report]."

This is then treated as a substitute motion—discussion and amendment are permitted first on the *committee report,* but no vote—then discussion and amendment permitted on the *substitute motion.* As in treating amendments, the vote is taken first on the minority amendment. If adopted, it replaces the "majority" motion which as *substituted* is put to the final vote. If the "minority" vote is defeated, the main motion (majority report) is put to vote.

COMMITTEE OF THE WHOLE
See RRO, p. 63

INFORMAL CONSIDERATION
See RRO, p. 65

Chapter XII

OFFICERS AND MEMBERS AND THEIR RESPECTIVE DUTIES

PRESIDENT
See RRO, pp. 77, 98

Duties

To acquire a working knowledge of parliamentary law and procedure and a thorough understanding of the constitution, bylaws, and standing rules of the organization.

Always to appear at the rostrum a few minutes before the meeting is scheduled to begin.

To have on hand a list of committees for a guide in naming new appointments.

To preside and maintain order.

To explain and decide all questions of order.

DUTIES OF OFFICERS & MEMBERS

To announce all business.

To be informed on communications.

To entertain only one main motion at a time and state all motions properly.

To permit none to debate motions before they are seconded and stated; to encourage debate and assign the floor to those properly entitled to it. (No member may speak twice on the same question if there are others who wish to claim the floor.)

To put all motions to vote and give result; to decide a tie vote or not to vote at all; to abstain from voting, if wiser.

To stand while stating the question and taking the vote.

To remain seated while discussion is taking place or reports are being given.

To enforce the rules of decorum and discipline.

To talk no more than necessary when presiding.

To refrain from discussing a motion when presiding.

To be absolutely fair and impartial.

To extend every courtesy to the opponents of a motion even though the motion is one that the presiding officer favors.

To give signature when necessary.

To be ex officio of all committees, except the nominating committee if so prescribed in bylaws.

To show appreciation to officers and chairmen of committees for devoted service.

To perform such other duties as are prescribed in the bylaws.

Privileges

To debate motions before the house, if essential, but must surrender the Chair until the vote has been taken. The vice-president is asked to take the Chair until motion has been disposed of.

To use "general consent," which saves much time when routine matters are considered. Form: "If there is no objection, we will . . ." If there is an objection, he must take the vote.

To preside during nominations and elections even if he is the candidate. When he is the sole nominee, merely out of a sense of delicacy, he permits the vice-president to put the question to a vote.

To sign checks, usually with the treasurer. One other

officer's name should be authorized in the event that the president or treasurer is unavailable.

VICE-PRESIDENT

In absence of the president, presides and performs the duties of president. If a vice-president is not willing to perform the duties of the president during his absence or when circumstances make it necessary to assume the presidency, the vice-president should resign from the office.

To head an important committee or share in supervising a department, as outlined in the bylaws.

RECORDING SECRETARY

To keep minutes of the meeting.

To take the roll call and mark the absentees at board meetings.

To read minutes of previous meeting (preferably standing).

To read important correspondence (or give the gist of it), if there is only one secretary.

To record the proceedings (what is done), not the debate (what is said).

To record the name of the member who introduced a motion. It is not necessary to record the seconder.

To notify committees of their appointments and business.

To take charge of all documents belonging to organization when requested.

To sign official documents of the society when requested.

To call a meeting to order, in the absence of the president or a vice-president, and to preside until the election of a chairman pro tem, which should take place immediately.

CORRESPONDING SECRETARY

To have a list of all officers, board members, and general membership.

To notify all members of meetings.

To conduct correspondence as directed.

To read important correspondence or the gist of it at meetings.

TREASURER

To receive and bank all moneys due the organization.
To keep bookkeeping records of such funds.

DUTIES OF OFFICERS & MEMBERS

To pay wherever possible by checks, countersigned by the president and himself.

To pay bills from officers and committee members only when clearly authorized and when receipts for expenditures are attached.

To disburse all moneys as the organization may direct.

To give a statement of finances as often as required.

To give a complete financial report, which has been audited, at annual meeting.

(An auditor or auditing committee's written report should be presented following the treasurer's report. Most organizations bond the treasurer and those entrusted with funds, when large sums are involved.)

ASSISTANT TREASURER OR FINANCIAL SECRETARY

To keep a record of all dues-paying members.

To send bills when due.

To make provision for collection of dues at meetings.

To turn over all collected moneys to the treasurer, giving an accurate record to the treasurer and keeping a duplicate for himself. This should be signed by the treasurer as having received such money. These records are to be kept by both for auditing purposes.

To report on status of paid-up membership at regular intervals.

Additional officers, elected or appointed, should be assigned such duties as the organization finds necessary.

DUTIES AND RIGHTS OF MEMBERS

Duties

To obtain the floor before speaking.

To stand when speaking, if convenient.

To avoid speaking upon any matter until it is properly brought before the house by a motion.

To keep upon the question then pending.

To yield the floor to calls for order.

To abstain from all personalities in debate.

To avoid disturbing, in any way, speakers of the assembly.

Rights

To offer any motion that is germane to the organization.

To explain or discuss that motion, or any matter properly before the meeting.

To call to order, if necessary. (A point of order can

interrupt a speaker. It is raised to ensure orderly procedure, particularly when there is a breach or violation of rules or bylaws, or when a member is not speaking on the motion before the house.)

To hold the floor, when legally obtained, until through speaking.

To appeal from the decision of the chair to that of the assembly.

Chapter XIII

THE MEETING WILL COME TO ORDER
See RRO, pp. 95, 98

AN EXAMPLE

This example of a meeting applies to organized groups with duly elected officers.

Meetings should be opened promptly at the hour stated (with ten or fifteen minutes grace at the most).

The presiding officer, hereinafter mentioned as the Chair, secures order by striking the gavel on the table and stating:

CHAIR: The meeting will please come to order. *(Taking note that a quorum is present.)* Mr. A. will lead us in prayer *(or the national anthem, salute to the flag, etc.).*

CHAIR: Will the secretary please read the minutes of the last meeting.

CHAIR: Thank you. Are there any corrections to the minutes?

MR. G., *a member raises his hand.*

CHAIR: Yes, Mr. G.?

MR. G: Mister Chairman, the name of Mr. H. has been left off the luncheon committee.

CHAIR: Thank you. If there are no objections, the minutes will be corrected to include the name of Mr. H. Will you make the correction, Mister Secretary? Any further corrections? If not, the minutes stand approved as corrected. *(If no corrections, "stand approved as read.")*

CHAIR *(to secretary)*: Is there any correspondence? Give us the gist of it.

CHAIR: We shall now hear the report of officers. *(Or board or executive committee, depending on who has a report.)*

If in addition to a report there are recommendations,

THE MEETING WILL COME TO ORDER

these matters, as well as correspondence and requests, may be dealt with quickly, or if they require general discussion and a motion, should be taken up under "new business."

CHAIR: Will the treasurer give us his report? Mr. B?

Cash on hand, receipts since last meeting, disbursements, etc.

CHAIR: Thank you. Are there any questions about the report? If not, the report will be filed for the auditor.

(The annual report is previously audited and then accepted.)

CHAIR: We will now call on the committee reports.

Standing committee reports. (Since time will not permit for all committees to report at one meeting, those most essential at the time should report. Committees should be informed in advance. If there are recommendations, these should be submitted as motions.)

Special committee reports.

CHAIR: Are there any questions? What is your pleasure concerning this information?

MR. L.: Mister Chairman, I move that we organize a choral group.

Seconded.

CHAIR: It has been moved and seconded that we organize a choral society. Any discussion?

After discussion, the Chair will proceed to put the motion to a vote. Those in favor of the motion will say "aye." Those opposed will say "no." The "ayes" have it, and the motion is carried, or the "noes" have it, and the motion is lost—depending on which side prevailed.

CHAIR: We shall now proceed to unfinished business.

Plans for a membership campaign. General discussion. Referred to a committee.

CHAIR: New business is now in order. Is there any new business before the house?

MR. M.: Mister Chairman: There was a request in the correspondence for a contribution to the Red Cross.

CHAIR: Thank you for reminding us.

MR. G.: I move that we contribute twenty-five dollars to the Red Cross.

MEMBER: I second it.

CHAIR: It has been moved and seconded that we contribute twenty-five dollars to the Red Cross. Any discussion?

Discussion.

MR. S.: Mister Chairman.

CHAIR: Yes, Mr. S.?

MR. S.: I move to amend the motion by striking out twenty-five dollars and inserting thirty-five dollars.

MEMBER: I second the amendment.

CHAIR: It has been moved and seconded to amend the motion to thirty-five dollars instead of twenty-five dollars. Any discussion?

Discussion pro and con.

MEMBER: I move the previous question. *Close debate.*

MEMBER: Seconded.

CHAIR: It has been moved and seconded to adopt the previous question. *(This requires a two-thirds vote and is undebatable.)* All in favor say "Aye" . . . those opposed say "No." . . . The "ayes" have it. We will now proceed to vote on the amendment "to change from twenty-five dollars to thirty-five dollars." All in favor of the amendment will say "Aye." . . . Those opposed, say "No" . . . The "Ayes" have it, and the amendment is passed. We must now vote on the main motion as amended. It has been moved and seconded that we contribute thirty-five dollars to the Red Cross. Any further discussion? All in favor, say . . ." *(etc.)*

CHAIR: This completes the business of the meeting. Are there any announcements?

Announcements.

Good and Welfare (or Good of the Order) if time permits. This gives members an opportunity to make constructive suggestions or express pleasure at certain undertakings or offer constructive criticism, etc. Sometimes motions are allowed if they do not pertain to any of the previous business.

The program (if arranged). The program is generally part of the meeting; the president or program chairman presides. The performers are thanked.

Since there is nothing further before the house, there is adjournment by the president.

The meeting is adjourned.

STANDARD AGENDA FOR REGULAR MEETINGS

Meeting called to order by president. (The meeting may be opened with prayer, national anthem, flag salute, etc., or purely business.) Extend greeting.

Minutes of previous meeting read by secretary. (Approved as read or corrected.)

Correspondence reported by secretary. (Motions arising out of correspondence may be taken up immediately or held over for new business.)

Report of board of directors. Place opposite the name of person to report. Take up recommendations or motions.

Report of treasurer.

Standing committees reports (enter all names to report), and general business that will be taken up.

Special committees reports (same procedure).

Special orders, if any.

Unfinished business. Itemize.

New business. Itemize.

Controlled announcements, whenever convenient.

The program (if there is one). This is part of the meeting. The program chairman or president presides (optional).

Adjournment by the president.

AGENDA FOR SPECIAL MEETING

The agenda is restricted to only such business that appears in the call of the meeting, unless these words are included in the call: "and such other business as may properly come before it."

SUGGESTED AGENDA FOR ANNUAL MEETING

Reading of minutes of previous monthly meeting (or may be dispensed with).

Annual reports: (all should be written).

Officers, if they have reports.

Treasurer.

Standing committees.

Resolutions, if any.

Amendments to constitution and bylaws, if any.

President (review of year's activities and those in the making).

Nomination and election of officers (nominations may be held at the previous month's meeting).

Greetings from the newly elected president.

Program.

Adjournment by president.

See your bylaws for specific instructions or rules concerning annual meeting.

Chapter XIV

MINUTES
See RRO, pp. 80, 101

The minutes of an organization are the official record of all business transacted, activites undertaken, plans projected, general growth, etc. The minutes should contain what is done and not what is said. They should be written in the third person. Minutes should include:

The name of the organization, date, place, and time of meeting.

Whether it was a regular or special meeting.

Names of president and recording secretary or their substitutes. The minutes should state whether those of the previous meeting were read and approved or if reading was dispensed with.

All main motions, whether adopted or lost. (A motion that was withdrawn should not be recorded.) Resolutions adopted should be entered in full.

The names of the persons making the motions, but the name of the seconder need not be recorded.

Points of order and appeals, whether sustained or lost.

Summarized reports of committees, unless written reports are appended.

All appointments of committees, elected delegates, etc.

When a count has been ordered, or where the vote is by ballot or roll call, the number of votes on each side should be recorded.

Time of adjournment.

Minutes should be signed by secretary. "Respectfully submitted" not used. Then: Approved ———— date and initials.

If corrected, correction made on right margin where needed and then stated in the minutes when corrected, at the next meeting.

Personal opinions of praise or criticism should not be recorded.

Some organizations prefer fuller minutes, particularly when they are mailed out to board members of state or national groups who wish to be better informed. But an average group may like its minutes fuller; reading the minutes highlights the previous meeting for the members absent at that meeting.

The minutes may be corrected whenever an error is noticed regardless of the time that has elapsed; but after their adoption, when too late to reconsider the vote, they require a two-thirds vote for their amendment, unless previous notice of the proposed amendment has been given; then only a majority vote is required.

Chapter XV
PARLIAMENTARY DON'TS

DON'TS FOR THE PRESIDING OFFICER

Don't fail to start the meeting on time (a quorum being present)—ten minutes grace may be allowed. If no quorum is present, start the meeting anyhow; the business will be held over until later when late arrivals will make up the quorum. The membership will take note that meetings start on time and will respond accordingly.

Don't stand during debate or while a report is being given.

Don't take part in debate while you are in the Chair. If you must speak, turn the chair over to the vice-president; do not return to the Chair until the vote has been taken.

Don't allow members to deal in personalities while debating.

Don't say "I think," "I appoint," "It's my opinion," etc., but say "The Chair thinks," "The Chair appoints," "It is the opinion of the Chair," etc.

Don't say "You are out of order," when you mean "The motion is out of order."

Don't strike with the gavel any harder than necessary to attract the attention of the members. Standing very quietly may accomplish surprising results.

Don't lose your calmness, objectivity, or impartiality.

DON'TS FOR MEMBERS

Don't be late for the meeting. You may be needed to complete a quorum.

Don't sit in the rear. Leave the rear seats for the late ones.

Don't say "I move you." Omit the "you."

Don't say "I make a motion to," say "I move to" . . .

Don't wait to obtain the floor in order to second a motion.

Don't stand while another is speaking.

Don't fail to take part in the debate if you have a viewpoint to express, or want information or parliamentary assistance.

Don't claim the floor the second time if there are others who wish to speak the first time.

Don't be silent during the debate and then criticize after the meeting.

Don't speak on a motion while the vote is being counted or taken.

Don't address a woman chairman as chairlady—say "Madam Chairman."

Don't carry on a conversation with your neighbor while someone is speaking.

Don't forget to notify the chairman of a committee of which you are a member if you cannot attend a committee meeting.

Don't delay paying your dues on time.

Don't accept an office unless you are willing to assume the responsibilities of the office.

Don't use your knowledge of parliamentary law to hinder business by constantly raising points of order, and insisting upon the strict observance of every rule at a meeting in which the majority of the members have no knowledge of these rules.

Don't leave the meeting, unless necessary, until the president declares the meeting adjourned. You may be needed for the quorum, or something very important may come up at the last moment.

Chapter XVI

SPEAKERS ARE HUMAN

There are speakers who give their services on a voluntary basis; others are paid lecturers. Some represent national groups or special causes and are earnest and dedicated volunteers. The professional speakers are usually authorities in their field or entertainers, etc. All should be treated with courtesy and consideration. When inviting a speaker, give him or her general information about the group, several dates to choose from if possible, the time, the place, the subject, how long to speak, and whether there will be a question and answer period after the talk. Also if there is to be a fee, mention the sum; if not, make it clear your understanding of this fact.

Secure some biographical material and photographs for publicity. The former also is needed in preparing the introduction.

If the speaker is from out of town, find out the time of arrival; a member of the program committee should meet the speaker on arrival, when possible. If he arrives some time before the meeting, the speaker should meet the president or be ushered to the place where he will remain until the meeting commences.

Begin the meeting on time, and if there is business, make it as brief as possible. Don't keep the speaker waiting long after the time scheduled. Many speakers are presented so late that they have neither the inclination nor time to do justice to the subject. Make your introduction short but warm and gracious. An introduction is not a speech and should be brief and to the point. One cannot mention all that is in the biographical sketch, but one can take out the highlights in a speaker's background, and explain his authority to speak on the subject. An appropriate personal anecdote may fit in. If the speaker is well-known to the audience, he is "presented"; if he is not known, he is "introduced." If a question period is planned, it helps to have a few "prompted" questions to get started.

Once again, be brief in thanking him with a few well-chosen words. Do not review his speech. The applause of the audience usually gives the reaction to the speaker. If the program chairman is presiding, the president may add a few gracious words and then quickly adjourn the meeting.

Arrange for transportation for the speaker. The next day, write him a note of appreciation.

Chapter XVII

NOMINATIONS AND ELECTIONS
See RRO, pp. 50, 73, 88

NOMINATIONS

The *nominations and elections of officers* require serious thought, for they are one of the most important facets of the organization's life. They do not receive the consideration which their importance merits even in parliamentary law sources.

The method of nominating and electing should be provided for in the bylaws of each organization, and should be consistently followed through. If the method is not provided for, nominations may be made from the floor, by a nominating committee, by ballot, or by mail, depending on the method adopted at a meeting of the assembly. The most usual practice is the appointment or election of a *nominating committee*. Many organizations have changed the ruling of a president serving ex-officio on all committees to that of "except the nominating committee."

The president does not appoint the entire nominating committee; he appoints two or three members, and the others are elected from the board and the membership. This makes for more objectivity and democracy. The first one named may be the chairman, or the committee may elect its chairman. A goodly number may be five or seven, except for state and national groups, when, in addition, geographical areas are represented. Many organizations have the chairman on nominations or a committee as a standing committee for the year, to have ample opportunity to study potential nominees.

The *nominating committee chairman* should not do the work of the committee over the telephone unless distance precludes, and then special arrangements should be made with the telephone company, whereby a meeting can be held over the phone. A meeting or, sometimes, several meetings are required where the majority of the committee must be present to give serious thought to the officers to be chosen, to give consideration to the best-qualified people available for office.

An objective way for each member of the nominating committee to give free expression to an opinion is for the chairman to pass slips of paper around and ask each committee member to write down the choice for president. These are *nominations only,* and form the basis for general discussion of the merits of the candidates, etc. When the final decision must be made, again a ballot should be taken for electing the candidate at the committee meeting. This secrecy has become essential to the free expression of choices. Having freely discussed the various candidates, the majority voting opinion is the prevailing one. The next step is to find out the availability of the candidates.

Members of the committee *may* be candidates, but if they are chosen for an office, it would be in good taste to resign from the nominating committee and be replaced.

The nominating committee is then prepared to give its report at the scheduled meeting for nominations of officers, or for board of directors, etc. In some groups, the nominating committee is given the authority to choose chairmen of standing committees. Many groups have nominations given at one meeting and elections at another. This permits the nominations from the floor to be included on the ballot to be prepared for the election meeting. The ballot is usually arranged alphabetically with the report of the nominating committee given first, and then those nominated from the floor. This is not obligatory, but many wish to be guided by the committee's report.

The American Institute of Parliamentarians reports that it frequently enters the names of the directors to be elected from the *end* of the alphabet arrangement *forward*, because there is a tendency to elect the first names on the ballot.

In accordance with the provisions of the bylaws, many groups, particularly state and national, place two or more candidates for each office on the slate, which leads to an exciting, contested election. The rules for such nominations are clearly defined. Unless restricted in the bylaws, members have the privilege of writing in names on the ballot (not nominated). Also, unless restricted, nominations may come from the floor, some require a certain number to endorse the nomination. In the regular procedure, a nomination requires no seconding.

In larger groups, it is customary for someone to make a motion to close nominations. But if nominations are not restricted in the bylaws, this motion is *not* in order until a reasonable time has been given for making nominations. The Chair inquires if there are any other nominations, and then places the motion or merely states, if there is no response, that the nominations are closed. This is done with each office.

Example: When the chairman of nominations is called

upon for its report or its ticket, and the slate has been given in its entirety, the presiding officer says: "You have heard the report of the committee. For president, the committee has nominated Mr. A. Are there further nominations for the office of president?" Additional nominations in accordance with constitutional rules may then be proposed. Time must be given for such nominations. Then the president states: "There being no further nominations, the nomination for president is closed. The next office is that of vice-president. The committee has nominated Mr. B. Are there any further nominations for the office of vice-president?" And so on down the line.

It is assumed that the consent of all nominees to serve has been secured before proposing the names.

ELECTIONS

When nominations have been completed, the assembly proceeds to the election, *voting* by the method prescribed in the constitution and bylaws. If for any reason it is desired to reopen nominations, it may be done by a majority vote; the motion is undebatable.

Election by ballot is preferable, as the ballot allows the members to vote in secrecy. A fair and impartial *election committee* is appointed earlier, and it is the duty of the *chairman of elections* to see that ballots and pencils, prepared in advance of the meeting, are ready for the election.

When the vote is by ballot, the president writes his ballot and casts it with the rest.

In large groups, state or national, a special election place is arranged, and voters carefully checked.

The *tellers' report* is prepared from a vote *tally sheet* listing candidates to the left and running a tally of fives to the right for quick count. After the ballots have been counted, the chairman of elections brings in the report.

The tellers' report should contain the number of votes cast, the number necessary for election, the number of votes received by each candidate, and the number of illegal votes. Votes should be credited to a candidate when the intent of the voter is clear. One ballot containing two for Mr. X., folded together, is rejected as fraudulent.

The chairman again reads the report of the tellers and declares who are elected. If the bylaws call for a majority vote in elections instead of a plurality vote, the winning candidate must have at least one more than half the votes cast, ignoring blanks, etc.

The tally sheet with the ballots are placed in a sealed envelope, signed by the tellers, and turned over to the secretary to retain until it is certain the assembly will not order a recount.

The newly elected president is presented and given the opportunity for a word of greeting and appreciation, but the outgoing officers continue until the end of the business meeting or until such time as may be specified in the bylaws.

Newly elected officers usually take over immediately at the end of the meeting without waiting for the installation, which may be arranged for a later date (unless the bylaws state otherwise).

The same rules apply if the election is held over for the following month.

National organizations should schedule their nominations and elections for at least the day preceding their last day of the convention. This will allow ample time for ballots to be prepared and, more important, for delegates to participate fully in this important duty. The nominating committee can report in the morning and the election held in the afternoon. Convention rules in the program should state when polls are open and when closed, and where they are, proper measures should be taken to safeguard the rights of delegates.

SAMPLE BALLOT

——— Federation of Men's Clubs

Election of Officers and Board of Directors

Date of Meeting

Mark X next to the name desired

PRESIDENT
Vote for 1
☐ Mr. A.

VICE-PRESIDENTS
Vote for 3
[or whatever number constitution provides]
☐ Mr. B.
☐ Mr. C.
☐ Mr. D.

BOARD OF DIRECTORS
Vote for 15
[usually have more listed names than number to be voted for]
☐ Mr. H.
☐ Mr. I.
☐ Mr. J.
☐ etc.
☐ etc.
☐ etc.
(OTHER OFFICERS IF NECESSARY)

TREASURER
Vote for 1
☐ Mr. E.

CORRESPONDING SECRETARY
Vote for 1
☐ Mr. F.

RECORDING SECRETARY
Vote for 1
☐ Mr. G.

NOMINATING COMMITTEE
[optional]
Mr. L., chairman

_____
_____
_____
_____

You are at liberty to name several candidates for the same position if organization authorizes.

Many organizations mail the ballot to the membership with the notice of the annual meeting, thus giving them information in advance.

Chapter XVIII

CONVENTIONS—ANNUAL, BIENNIAL, OR TRIENNIAL—OF NATIONAL, FEDERATED BODIES WITH LOCAL CHAPTERS

A convention is a gathering of organized constituent groups, all paid-up members, which are usually registered members of the national organization. All participating units are given proportionate representation by properly elected delegates, who have authority to vote on important questions and issues coming before the convention. Actions taken by such conventions are usually binding on their component units. Delegates are expected to report back at their meetings a résumé of the actions taken and their impressions of the proceedings.

Conventions usually supply much information and inspiration. The opportunity to meet co-workers from all over makes for fine relationships and gives added incentive for continuing activities.

Conventions of state, regional, or national organizations, in many instances, have become grandiose affairs, frequently without sufficient time to do justice to their problems and issues.

The primary purpose of such conventions is to permit the organization's constituency, through its delegates, to assume greater responsibility in reviewing its policies, its projects, its actions since the preceding convention, and to assume further responsibilities in carrying through the objectives of the organization. (The business of many conventions is limited to specific items in their bylaws.)

Conventions of a more formal nature are elaborate with much entertainment, luncheons and formal dinners, exhibits, etc. Committees are appointed long in advance—programming, publicity, printing, transportation, hotel accommodations, hospitality, information, registration, credentials, etc.

The constitution usually provides for national officers, chairmen of standing committees, and directors of the board to be ex officio delegates of the convention with full rights. Provision is also made for the proportionate representation of delegates from the local units, usually to be elected at local meetings so designated for the purpose. (Names and addresses of elected delegates are sent to the national office.) A registration fee is charged for all delegates, and often for alternates and guests to help defray the expenses of the convention.

Previous to the opening of the convention, delegates register at designated stations and receive their kits, which include a program, reports, general information, badge, and often a credential card—sometimes souvenirs, etc. The convention is officially opened with appropriate exercises by dignitaries of the organization, city, celebrities, etc., in keeping with the character of the organization. At the opening of the business session, the president calls the meeting to order. The credentials chairman is called upon for a report of the registered delegates. A motion is made to accept the report. Supplementary reports are given as delegates arrive later. The next order of business is the report of the program chairman, who submits the printed program. He or someone else moves its adoption. This is open to debate and amendment, and, when once adopted by a majority vote, cannot be deviated from except by a two-thirds vote of those voting.

Additional reports may be required from the program chairman, because changes in the program may be necessary due to the unavoidable absence of speakers, etc. The agenda usually includes the president's address (it may have been given at the opening meeting), reports of the board, standing committees (these reports are usually printed and not read, to save time), treasurer's report (may be printed, but usually read), report of the nominating committee, election of officers, acceptance of a budget (often increased), acceptance of new projects, resolutions, amendments to constitution and bylaws, and/or such other business as has been adopted.

During the convention period, separate meetings may be held of the board, committee chairmen with their local chairmen, workshops, etc.

The election of the officers should be held the day before the last day of the convention to allow for sufficient time and when most of the delegates will be present. The last day usually allocated for elections and important business deprives the delegates of their rights, since many must check out of hotels or be tied up with plane arrangements.

The term of office for elected officers begins at the close of the convention, to allow the same officers to serve throughout the meetings. But the newly elected officers should be presented, and the new president extend a few gracious remarks.

Sometimes an installation is arranged as an inspiring ceremony.

Frequently, the new officers and directors remain to hold a special meeting for new plans to be considered.

In federated national organizations, the rules and policies adopted at conventions become the rulings for all bodies.

Since a convention is the supreme authority for the organization, no body or executive committee can repeal, rescind, reconsider, or otherwise modify or change any act or vote of a superior body.

(While the rules require that at the beginning of the meetings each day the minutes of the preceding day are read and approved, it seems that this is honored in the breach rather than in the practice. Since large conventions engage stenotypists or tape the proceedings, they are not prepared in time. It is advisable to give the authority for editing and approving the minutes to the board or a special committee. The proceedings or excerpts are then published and sent out to the constituent groups. The minutes of a previous convention are not read nor should any action be taken on them. Each convention must attend to its own minutes.)

Chapter XIX
SOME USEFUL MISCELLANEOUS INFORMATION

POINTERS FOR THE PRESIDENT

On election to the presidency, the president should meet with his officers and discuss plans for the months ahead. They should be made to feel that their help is desired, and they should be consulted in considering the standing committee chairmen to be appointed. Vice-presidents should be given definite commitments. Then as early as possible, a meeting should be held with the standing committee chairmen, the work of the committees explained, and also, if time permits, future plans under these committees discussed. Former officers and chairmen, if invited, could contribute by pooling their experiences.

A schedule should be prepared of a calendar of events arranged by months and all important dates, holiday events, special functions, conferences, courtesy attendances at meetings of other organizations, etc.—all listed in chronological order. This will avoid conflict of dates. Under these dates, list what needs to be done. All this will help toward working in an organized way and getting activities started in plenty of time.

Many clubs print yearbooks with advertising that pays for the printing. The yearbook contains interesting information about the club, lists important dates, members and their telephone numbers; it serves as a valuable directory of the members.

Be thoroughly familiar with your constitution and bylaws and abide by them. Also become knowledgeable about parliamentary procedure, so that your meetings may run smoothly, expeditiously, and with decorum and dignity.

In preparation for the next meeting, the minutes of the previous meeting should be gone over with the secretary to correct them in advance, if necessary, and to be prepared with the order of business.

The experience gained in a short period gives one confidence, and proficiency in performing one's duties.

RELATIONSHIPS

In choosing officers for an organization, a voluntary one, which holds meetings monthly, it helps to elect those on friendly terms with the president, who should be in close contact with them and consult them and meet frequently for plans to be considered. Their goodwill and cooperation are essential to the success of the organization.

Much needs to be said about the relationship between a past president and an incoming president. Though many presidents are glad to be relieved of their responsibility and of undue criticism at times on the part of members, there are many who have enjoyed prestige and power and cannot graciously relinquish it. Such presidents may frequently make it difficult for their successors. "This is not the way we did it" is often the interruption at meetings, and it becomes embarrassing when issues are publicly debated.

The importance of limiting term in office has been too well demonstrated to require more on the subject. It is only in the last twenty years that some national organizations have written into their constitutions a definite limitation of term for their officers and particularly for the president.

Some organizations have written into their bylaws that the past president should take a recess for a year— the past president is not allowed on the organization's board—but this is a very drastic and unwarranted measure.

It is assumed that the cause should be of far more

importance and that zealous workers can overcome personal interests for the greater good.

Outgoing presidents should make their exit graciously and take over an important chairmanship to assist the new administration and to set an example to the other workers.

SOCIAL FUNCTIONS—GUEST SEATING AND PROTOCOL

All organized clubs and particularly women's clubs make much of social functions in the form of luncheons and dinners. The question of honoring key workers at a head table becomes a difficult one, particularly in a large chapter with many area groups in the same city. Many clubs have to resort to two head tables on different levels on the platform or in different parts of the room.

The problem is further complicated if the chapter belongs to a national organization, and many of the officers and national committee chairmen may live in the same city. If the function is held by the national leadership, a conference or convention, they honor their own key members and include the president of the local group. The same holds true for regional and state affairs; their officers are in command. When it is a local function, the local officers and key chairmen are the honored guests, in addition to those specially invited as speakers, guests, etc. If a national president or national vice-president lives in the same city as the local chapter, national greetings would be expected; these national officers are always seated at the dais. But other national officers and national chairmen of committees could be placed at a "special" table directly in front of the center of the dais, and singled out by name with a few gracious remarks by the presiding chairman.

Those to be seated at the dais meet together in a reception room and march in shortly after the time scheduled for the function to begin. Place cards should be used, and the line usually forms in that arrangement.

The president is not always the presiding chairman, but he should extend greetings (unless he is one of the speakers) and present the presiding chairman. The president is seated in the center right whether or not he is the presiding chairman; if someone else is presiding, then the presiding chairman is seated in the center left, but the president always sits center right. The officers and special guest of honor are divided on either side in order of rank. Others take the second head table.

Usually, those on the platform are introduced from one end to the other, leaving out the speakers.

When a number of speakers and guests are seated at the head table, they are usually (though not necessarily) taken notice of by another speaker thus: "Mr. Chairman, Mr. ———, Mr. ———, distinguished guests, ladies and gentlemen," or "Mister President, Honored Clergy, Mayor... (mention other notable and distinguished guests), ladies and gentlemen..." The presiding officer is always mentioned first.

A uniform procedure should be worked out for functions so that a policy is established and can be followed consistently and objectively.

GENERAL

A president, knowing he will be absent from a future meeting, cannot authorize another member to act in his place at such meetings; a vice-president takes over. If there is no vice-president present, the recording secretary calls the meeting to order and presides, pending the election of a temporary presiding officer.

If a president is late for a meeting, the vice-president should start the meeting if a quorum is present. The president, upon arriving, should wait until the pending business is over before taking his seat.

All reports by officers and committees should be written in the third person.

If a society wishes to provide for honorary officers or members, it should do so only if provided for in the bylaws or by vote of the assembly. It should require a two-thirds or unanimous vote. This honorary membership can be rescinded.

An honorary office conferred on an active, dues-paying member in no way conflicts with holding a real office or being assigned any duty whatsoever.

In the absence of the president, the vice-president is not ex officio of any committee.

When a motion of thanks is given to a speaker or entertainer, the negative vote is never taken, as a matter of courtesy.

The principle that no officer should serve consecutively more than two or three years at the utmost in the same office is recommended. Rotation in office makes it possible to bring new personnel into leadership posts and to give a new approach to the activities and interests of the organization. Each person usually has his own following, and new leadership is developed, which usually strengthens the organization. If agreed upon, it should be in the bylaws. After the lapse of one term, he may be elected again to the same office.

A chairman should always be courteous and fair, but when the Chair is convinced that members are using parliamentary forms merely to obstruct business, he should either not recognize them or else rule them out of order.

Dilatory, absurd, or frivolous motions are not entertained.

Motions made as the result of board or committee meetings by their chairmen do not require a second. These motions represent the considered action of more than one member.

A caucus of members or delegates at a conference or convention to determine policies, to consider candidates, or united to take a test of their strength on a given proposal is in order and in keeping with the democratic process.

The most serious defect in most meetings is the lack of reasonable decorum. Good order must be maintained by the presiding officer if business is to be carried out. The gavel is the symbol of authority, but repeated rapping sometimes fails to restore order. The chairman should stand quietly and wait for silence. The membership usually stops talking to see what is going on. The chairman then resumes the business.

It is a mistaken courtesy to move "that an election be made unanimous." It forces those who did not vote for the candidate to submit unwillingly to the transferring of their vote, thus making it appear that it was unanimous when it was not. One negative vote defeats a motion to make the vote unanimous.

Any officer or chairman who submits a report with a recommendation should move its adoption before taking his seat. It does not require a second. The report should be in writing and given to the recording secretary.

The procedure for filling vacancies among the officers and members of the board should be specifically stated in the constitution. It is customary for a vice-president to fill the vacancy occurring in the office of president. But where there are a number of vice-presidents and no designated first vice-president, this presents a problem. With no provision made, the office of president should be filled by election by the board of directors—he serves only until the next annual meeting. This should also apply for vacancies occurring among the members of the board.

Quóting from RRO, p. 79 "A chairman will often find himself perplexed with the difficulties attending his position, and in such cases he will do well to heed the advice of a distinguished writer on parliamentary law, and recollect that 'The great purpose of all rules and forms is to subserve the will of the assembly rather than to restrain it; to facilitate, and not to obstruct, the expression of their deliberate sense.' "

BIBLIOGRAPHY

The Clubmember's Handbook, Lucy R. and Harold V. Milligan, New Home Library, New York, 1942.

Cushing's Manual of Parliamentary Practice, Luther S. Cushing, ed. Albert S. Bolles, Holt, Rinehart & Winston.

Davidson's Handbook of Parliamentary Procedure, Henry A. Davidson, Ronald Press Company, New York, 1955.

Demeter's Manual of Parliamentary Law and Procedure, George Demeter, Bostonia Press, Boston, 1953.

Parliamentary Journal, a quarterly publication of the American Institute of Parliamentarians, Chicago.

Robert's Rules of Order, General Henry M. Robert, Scott, Foresman & Company, Chicago, 1904.

Robert's Rules of Order Revised, General Henry M. Robert, Scott, Foresman & Company, New York, 1915.

Parliamentary Practice, General Henry M. Robert, The Century Company, New York, 1921.

Robert's Parliamentary Law, General Henry M. Robert, Appleton Century Crofts, Inc., New York, 1951.

Diagram of Parliamentary Motions in Order of Precedence

(Except for Incidental Motions, which have no rank among themselves)

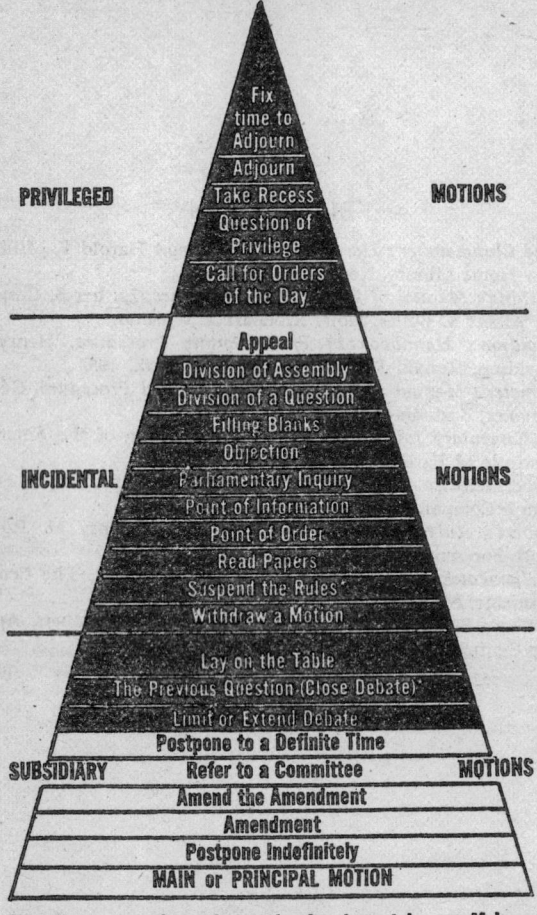

PRIVILEGED MOTIONS
- Fix time to Adjourn
- Adjourn
- Take Recess
- Question of Privilege
- Call for Orders of the Day

INCIDENTAL MOTIONS
- Appeal
- Division of Assembly
- Division of a Question
- Filling Blanks
- Objection
- Parliamentary Inquiry
- Point of Information
- Point of Order
- Read Papers
- Suspend the Rules
- Withdraw a Motion

SUBSIDIARY MOTIONS
- Lay on the Table
- The Previous Question (Close Debate)*
- Limit or Extend Debate
- Postpone to a Definite Time
- Refer to a Committee
- Amend the Amendment
- Amendment
- Postpone Indefinitely
- MAIN or PRINCIPAL MOTION

Miscellaneous motions after action has been taken on Main or Principal Motion: Take from Table (undebatable)
    Rescind (debatable)**
    Reconsider (debatable)
    Ratify (debatable)

White spaces—Debatable Motions. Black spaces—Undebatable Motions
* Motions requiring a two-thirds vote
** Requires two-thirds vote without notice and majority vote with notice

The chart at left is a diagram of parliamentary motions and gives the order of procedure. A presiding officer should have this in front of him as a guide in dealing with motions that are presented, so as to make it easier to know what to do with any kind of motion that may be presented.

Study it carefully, as it gives at a glance those motions which may take precedence over other motions made practically at the same time.

You will note that the Main or Principal Motion is at the bottom in rank. The other motions may be made while the Main Motion is pending, and must be dealt with before the Main Motion. They are arranged according to rank, the highest at the top of the list. Incidental motions, however, have no rank among themselves, yet take precedence over subsidiary motions. When any one motion is immediately pending, the motions above it on the list are in order and those below are out of order. A careful study will enable one to know which are debatable, undebatable, and which require a two-thirds vote instead of a majority vote.

INDEX

INDEX

The figures refer usually to where the treatment of the subject begins. Always consult the Table of Rules, p. 11, for information about any particular motion. A complete list of motions will be found in the Index, under the title, "Motions, list of." The arrangement of the work can be most easily seen by examining the Table of Contents [pp. 7-10]; its plan is explained in the Introduction, pp. 21-25.

                                                                          PAGE

Adjourn, motion to, ...33, 115
   effect upon unfinished business, ...33
   in committee [see, *Rise, motion to*] 33, 58, 63-64
   motion to "fix the time to which to adjourn" 33, 115

Adopt, Accept or Agree, ...60-61

Amendment, motion to "amend," 49, 108
   by "adding," or "inserting," 49
   by "striking out," 49, 108
   by "striking out and inserting," 49
   by "substituting," 49
   by "dividing the question," 30, 49
   of an amendment, ...49
   in committee, ...57, 104
   of reports or propositions with several
      paragraphs, ...62, 95
   of Rules of Order, By Laws and Constitutions, ...86
   motions that cannot be amended, ...12, 50-51, 108
   examples of improper amendments, ...50

Announcing the Vote, ...72, 73, 106

Appeal from the decision of the chair, ...37-38, 114

Apply, meaning of, ...24

189

	PAGE
Assembly, how organized,	88-96
the word to be replaced by Society, Convention, etc., when it occurs in forms of questions,	25
right to punish members,	119
right to eject persons from their room,	119-120
trial of members,	120

Ayes and Noes [same as *Yeas and Nays*], ... 74

Ballot, ... 73

Blanks, filling of, ... 50
   in balloting, not to be counted, ... 74

Boards, of Trustees, Managers, etc., reports of, in order when reports of standing committees are made, ... 86
[See *Quorum*].

Business, introduction of, ... 27-31, 105
   order of, ... 86
   priority of, questions relating to are undebatable, ... 67
   unfinished, effect of an adjournment upon, ... 33

By-Laws, what they should contain, ... 96-97
   adoption of, ... 95
   amendment of, ... 86-87
   suspension of [Note] 40

Call of the House, ... 122

Call to Order, ... 38, 114

Chairman, duties of, ... 77, 98-99
   election of, ... 88
   temporary, ... 78, 92
   right to vote when it affects result, ... 72, 77-78
   of a committee, ... 56, 104
   of committee of the whole, ... 63
   inexperienced, hints to, ... 99-100

Change of Vote allowed before result is announced, ... 72

Classification of Motions according to their object, ..106-107
   into Privileged, Incidental, Subsidiary and Principal 31-32

Clerk [see *Secretary*].

Close Debate, motion to, ... 70-71, 109-110

Commit, motion to, ... 47-48, 108

INDEX

Committees, appointment of, ... 48, 90-91
how they should be composed, ... 48, 104
chairman of, ... 56, 90, 100
object of, ... 56, 104, 108
quorum in, consists of a majority, ... 57, 85
quorum in Committee of the Whole, same in
    Assembly, ... 85
manner of conducting business in, ... 57, 104-105

Reports of, their form, ... 58-59, 105
    their reception, ... 59, 90-91
    their adoption, ... 60-61, 91
    their place in the order of business, ... 86
    common errors in acting [Note] 59-60
Minority Reports of, their form, ... 59, 105
    cannot be acted upon unless moved as a sub-
    stitute for the committee's (majority's)
    report, ... 57, 105
select and standing, distinction between, ... 56
of the whole, ... 63
as if in committee of the whole, ... 65

Congress, rules, of, the basis of this work, ... 22-23

Consent, unanimous [same as *General*], ... 40, 73-74
can be given only when a quorum is present [Note], ..85

Consideration of a question, objection to, ... 39, 111

Constitutions, what they should contain, ... 96-98
adoption of, by a society, ... 95-96
amendment of, ... 86-87
cannot be suspended [Note] 40

Convention, organizing and conducting a meeting of, 92-93

Credentials of delegates, ... 92

Debate, what precedes, ... 29-30, 105-106
no member to speak but twice in same, ... 66, 116
no speech to be longer than ten minutes, ... 66, 116
number and length of speeches in Congress
    [Note] 66-67, 116
member reporting measure has right to close, ... 66
list of *undebatable* question, ... 67-69
motions that open the main question to, ... 68
principles regulating the extent of, ... 68-69
decorum in, ... 69-70, 116

ROBERT'S RULES OF ORDER

PAGE

Debate, *continued.*
   closing, or limiting, ...70-71, 109-110
   limits of, can be extended by a ⅔ vote, ...66, 75

Decorum in debate, ...69-70, 116

Definitions of various terms, ...24-26

Delegates, organization of a meeting of, ...92-93

Dilatory motions not permitted, ...79

Disorderly words in debate, ...69-70

Division of the assembly, ...72
   of questions [see *Amendment*], ...30, 49-50, 108

Duties of Officers [see *Chairman, Secretary* and *Treasurer*].

Ecclesiastical Tribunals, legal rights of, ...120

Eject persons from their room, right of an
   assembly to, ...119-120

Election of Officers, ...88-89, 92-93

Errors, common, ...and notes on pp. 25-59, 79-80
   in amendments 51

Ex-officio [Note] 56

Explanation, personal, unprivileged [Note], ...115

Expulsion of Members requires a ⅔ vote, ...121

Expunge [Note] 52

Extend the limits of debate, ...66, 75, 116

Filling blanks, ...50

Fix the time to which to Adjourn, motion to, ...33, 115

Floor, how to obtain, ...27, 105-106
   necessary to obtain in order to make a motion 28-29

Forms of making motions, ...105-106
   of a resolution, ...105-106
   of stating and putting questions, ...14, 71, 117-118
   of announcing the result of a vote, ...72, 73, 106
   of acting on reports of committees, ...59, 61-63, 91
   of acting on reports or resolutions containing
      several paragraphs, ...62, 95-96

INDEX

Forms of making motions, *continued.*
of reports of committees, ...58-59, 105
of treasurer's reports, ...103-104
of minutes of a meeting, ...80-82, 101
of conducting an occasional or mass meeting, ...88 ff.
of conducting a meeting of delegates, ...92-93
of conducting a meeting to organize a society, ...93 ff.
of conducting an ordinary meeting of a society, ...94-96

General Consent [see *Consent, unanimous*].

Hints to Inexperienced Chairmen, ...99-100

House, call of the, ...122-124

Incidental questions, ...32

Indecorum, leave to continue speaking after, 38, 69-70, 114

Indefinite postponement, ...51, 111

Informal consideration of a question, ...65

Introduction of Business, ...27-31, 105-106

Journal [see *Minutes*].

Lay on the table, motion to, ...41-43, 109, 111

Legal Rights [see *Assembly* and *Ecclesiastical Tribunals*].

Limit debate, motion to, ...71, 76

Main question, ...31

Majority [see *Two-thirds and Quorum*].

Meeting, distinction between it and *session* [Note] 83
how to conduct [see *Forms*].

Members not to be present during a debate concerning themselves, ...70
not to vote on questions personal to themselves, ...72
trial of, ...120-122
not to be expelled by less than a two-thirds vote, ...121

Minority Report [see *Committees*].

Minutes, form and contents of, ...80-82, 100-101
correction of, ...81

Moderator [see *Chairman*].

Modification of a motion by the mover, ...29, 30, 40

PAGE

Motions, list of. [For details see each motion in the index].
adjourn, ...33, 115
adjourn, fix the time to which to, ...33, 115
adopt a report [same as *accept* or *agree to*], ...60-61, 91
amend, ...49, 108
appeal, ...87-38, 114
blanks, filling, ...50
call to order, ...38, 114
close debate, ...70-71, 109-110
commit, ...47-48, 108
consideration of a question, objection to, ...39, 111
divide the question, ...30, 49-50, 108
expunge [Note] 52
extend the limits of debate, ...66, 75, 116
fix the time to which to adjourn, ...33, 115
incidental motions or questions, ...32
indefinitely postpone, ...51, 111
Informal consideration of a question, ...65
lay on the table, ...41-43, 109, 111
leave to continue speech when guilty
  of indecorum, ...38, 69-70, 114
leave to withdraw a motion, ...40
limit debate, ...70-71, 110
main motions or questions, ...31
objection to the consideration of a question, ...39, 111
order, questions of, ...38, 114
orders of the day, ...85-37, 113
orders, special, ...36, 113
postpone to a certain day, ...47, 108-109
postpone indefinitely, ...51, 111
previous question, ...43 ff., 109-110
principal motions or questions 31
priority of business, questions relating to, ...67
privileged motions or questions, ...32
privilege, questions of, ...35, 115
reading papers, ...39
reception of a report [see *Committees*], ...59, 90-91
recommit [same as Commit], ...47-48, 108
reconsider, ...53 ff., 112-113
refer [same as Commit], ...47-48, 108
renewal of a motion, ...52, 113
rescind, ...52
rise [in committee, equals adjourn], ...33, 58, 63-65

Motions, list of, *continued.*
  shall the question be considered [or discussed]? 39, 111
  special order, to make a, ...36, 113
  strike out [see *Amendment*], ...49, 108
  subsidiary motions or questions, ...31
  substitute [one form of *Amendment*, which see] 49, 108
  suspension of the Rules, ...40, 114
  take from the table [see *Lay on the Table*],...........41, 109
  take up a question out of its proper order, ...86
  withdrawal of a motion, ...40

Motions, Table of Rules relating to, ...12-14
  classified according to their object, ...107
  classified into Privileged, Incidental,
      Subsidiary, etc., ...31-32
  order of precedence of [see each motion, §§ 10-27], ...14
  how to be made, ...27-30, 88 ff., 105-106
  a second required [with certain exceptions] 29, 117
  to be stated by chairman before being discussed ..29, 106
  when to be in writing, ...30, 105
  how to be divided, ...30, 49
  how to be modified by the mover, ...30-31, 40
  how to be stated and put to the question 71, 117-118
  that are in order when another has the floor, ...28-29
  that do not have to be seconded, ...30
  that *cannot be amended,* 12, 50-51, 180
  that *cannot be debated,* 67-69
  that open main question to debate, ...68
  that require two-thirds vote for their adoption, ...75-77
  dilatory, not allowed, ...79

Nominations, how treated, ...50, 88-89
  closing, effect of, ...73

Numbers of paragraphs, clerk to correct, without a vote, 50

Objection to the consideration [discussion or introduction] of a question, ...39, 111

Obtaining the floor 27

Officers of an assembly [See *Chairman, Secretary, Treasurer* and *Vice-President*].
  election of, ...88-89
  temporary, ...91-92

PAGE

Order, questions of and a call to, ...38, 114
  of business, ...86
  of the day, ...35-37, 113
  special, ...36, 113
  of precedence of motions [see *Precedence*].

Organization of an occasional or mass meeting, ...88 ff
  of a convention or assembly of delegates, ...92-93
  of a permanent society, ...93 ff.

Papers and documents, reading of, ...39
  in custody of Secretary, ...82, 101

Parliamentary Law, its origin, etc., ...21-22

Personal explanation, not privileged [Note] 115

Plan of the Manual, ...23-25

Postpone to a certain time, ...47, 108-109
  indefinitely, ...51, 111

Preamble, considered after the rest of a paper, ...62

Precedence of motions [see each motion, §§ 10-27], ...14
  meaning of, ...24

Presiding Officer [see *Chairman*].

Previous question, ...43 ff., 109-110

Principal (or main) question, ...31

Priority of Business, questions relating to, are
  undebatable, ...67

Privilege, questions of, ...35, 115

Privileged questions, ...32

Programme of a meeting [same as *orders of the day*] 36

Putting the question, form of, ...71, 118

Questions [see *Forms, Motions, Privilege, Privileged,*
  ***Order, Stating* and *Putting*].**

Quorum, when there is no rule, consists of a majority, ...85
  committees and boards cannot decide upon, ...85
  in Congress and Parliament [Note], ...85

INDEX

	PAGE
Reading of Papers,	39
Reception of a report [see *Committees*],	59
Recess,	34-35
Recommit [same as Commit],	47-48, 108
Reconsider,	53 ff., 112-113
Record, or minutes,	80-82, 100-101

Recording officer [see *Secretary*].

Refer [same as Commit],	47-48, 108
Renewal of a motion,	52, 113

Reports of committees [see *Committees*].

Rescind,	52
Resolutions, forms of,	105-106
not in order if they conflict with Constitution, By-Laws or Rules of Order,	98

Rights of assemblies [see *Assembly*].

of ecclesiastical tribunals,	120
Rise, motion to, in committee, equals adjourn,	33, 58, 63-65
Rules of Debate [see *Debate*],	66-71, 116-117
of Order, amendment of,	86-87
of Order, what they should contain,	97-98
standing, what they should contain,	98
suspension of,	40, 114
relating to motions, Table of,	12-14
Seconding, motions that do not require,	30, 117
Secretary, duties of,	80, 100
additional duties of, when receiving money,	101-102
election of,	88-89
Session,	83-85
Shall the question be considered [or discussed]?	39, 111
Speaking, Rules of [see *Debate*],	66-67, 69-70, 116
Special Order,	36, 113

	PAGE
Standing Rules,	98
Stating a Question, form of,	71, 117-118
Strike Out [see *Amendment*]	49, 108
Subsidiary motions or questions,	31
Substitute [see *Amendment*]	49, 108
Sum, smallest, first put,	50
Suspension of the Constitution or By-Laws [Note],	40
of the Rules,	40, 114
of the Standing Rules,	40, 98
Table of Rules, relating to motions,	12-14
Table, motion to lay on the,	41-43, 109, 111
motion to take from the,	41
Tellers,	72, 73
Time, longest, first put,	50
Treasurer, duties of,	102-104
Trial of Members,	120-122
Two-thirds vote, motions requiring,	75
various kinds of, explained [Note],	75
principles regulating [Note],	75

Unanimous Consent, [see *Consent, Unanimous*].

Undebatable Questions,	67-69
Unfinished Business, effect of adjournment upon,	33-34
its place in the order of business,	86
Vice-Presidents,	91-92
Vote, various methods of putting the question,	71, 117-118
various methods of voting,	71-74
forms of announcing,	71, 73, 74, 106
change of, permitted before result is announced,	72
effect of a tie,	73
motions requiring more than a majority,	75
plurality,	72
chairman entitled to when it affects result,	72, 77-78

	PAGE
Whole, Comittee of the,	63
Withdrawal of a Motion,	40
Yeas and Nays, voting by,	74
Yields, meaning of,	24

INDEX FOR: GUIDE AND COMMENTARY by Rachel Vixman

Accept, Adopt, Approve, ...152

Adjourn, ...133, 142, 143, 144, 152, 164, 165, 168

Agenda [see *Business*], ...153
    for Regular Meetings, ...164
    for Special Meeting, ...165
    for Annual Meeting, ...165
    for Conventions, ...176
    Special, ...165

Amend, Amendments, ...135, 137-138, 142, 143, 146,
                                          152, 164, 165, 176
    Primary, ...138
    Secondary, ...138

Appeal, ...134, 141, 142, 143, 162

Assembly [see *House*], ...152, 153, 161, 162
    Division of, ...134, 142, 143, 144, 152

Ballot, ...145, 149, 171, 172
    Sample, ...173-174
    Mailing of, ...174

Board of Directors [same as *Executive Board*,
    Trustees, Managers], ...148, 149-150, 155-156,
                                                   160, 165, 182
    Annual reports of, ...165

Business, ...152, 159, 160, 164
    New, ...163, 165
    Special order of, ...144, 165
    Unfinished, ...163, 165

	PAGE
By-Laws,	132, 134n., 144, 146-147, 148, 152, 155, 158, 159, 160, 162, 165, 170, 171, 172, 173, 178, 180
Caucus,	181
Chair, Chairman,	132, 133, 149, 151, 152, 155, 159, 162-164, 170-172, 181
Voting,	146
Pro tem,	160
Decision of,	162
Don'ts for,	167
of elections,	172
Commit [see *Refer*],	135, 152, 153, 157
Committees,	142, 144, 147-148, 149, 157, 160, 168
Election,	172
Executive,	156, 162
Nominating,	170-171, 173
of the whole,	158
Special,	157, 163, 165
Standing,	156-157, 163, 165
Constitution,	144, 146-147, 152, 158, 178, 181
Conventions,	173, 174-177
Delegates to,	174-175
Correspondence,	159, 160, 162, 163, 165
Debate,	131, 152, 159, 161, 164, 167, 168, 176
Limit or extend,	135, 143, 144
Depose from office,	144
Elections,	144-145, 159, 172-174, 176
Executive Board [see *Board of Directors*].	
Ex-officio,	152, 159, 170, 175, 180
Expel,	144
Filling blanks,	134, 139, 142, 143
Financial report,	161, 163
Fiscal year,	152
Floor,	152, 159, 160, 161, 168
General consent,	145, 146, 152, 159

INDEX TO GUIDE AND COMMENTARY

PAGE

Germane, ...152, 161

Good and Welfare (Good of the Order), ...152, 164

House [see *Assembly*].

Inquiries, ...142, 143

Installation, ...173, 176

Lay on the table, ...135, 137, 142, 143, 144, 147

Managers, [see *Board of Directors*].

Members' duties and rights, ...161-162
    Don'ts for, ...167-168

Minutes, ...143, 146, 148, 149-150, 153, 160,
                      162, 164, 165, 177, 178
    Contents of, ...166-167

Motions [see *Resolutions*], ...131-132, 133, 135, 138,
                     149, 159, 161, 165, 168, 180
    Debatable, ...145, 183
    Diagram of precedence, ...183
    Dilatory and frivolous, ...140, 141, 181
    Incidental, ...133-134, 135, 183
    Principal (Main), ...131, 133, 142, 144, 149,
                              153, 164, 183
    Privileged, ...132-133, 135, 183
    Rank of, ...135-136, 141, 148
    Secondary, ...132, 149
    Subsidiary, ...135, 183
    Substitute, ...138
    Summary of facts about, ...141-145
    Table, ...154
    Undebatable, ...140n., 143, 145, 164, 172
    Withdrawal of, ...134, 142, 143

Nominations, ...142, 143, 144, 148-149, 159, 165, 169-172
    Chairman of, ...170-171
    Close, ...134, 171-172
    from floor, ...170, 171
    Reopen, ...134, 172

Objection, ...144

Orders of the day, ...133, 141, 142, 143, 144, 145, 153

Parliamentarians, ...150-151, 153
    American Institute of, ...177

	PAGE
Parliamentary, inquiry,	133, 134, 142, 144
Law,	153, 168
Procedure,	130, 178
Pending,	153
Plurality,	153
Point of information,	142, 143
Point of order,	133, 134, 141, 142, 143, 145, 153, 162, 168
Polls,	143
Postpone,	135
Indefinitely,	135, 137, 142, 145, 153
Preamble,	153
Precedence,	153
President,	156, 160, 164, 165, 169, 170, 173, 179, 180, 181-182
Duties of,	158, 159
Pointers for,	177-178
Privileges of,	159-160
Prevailing side,	153
Pro tem,	153, 160
Question,	131, 144, 153, 159, 161
Division of,	134, 142, 143, 144, 152
Objection to consideration of,	134, 137, 142, 143
Previous,	135, 142, 143, 144, 147, 153, 164
Quorum,	132, 134, 141, 143, 153, 162, 167, 168, 180
Ratify,	140, 141
Read papers,	134, 142
Recess,	133, 143, 144, 153
Reconsider,	140, 141, 142, 143, 144, 145
Refer [see *Commit*].	
Relationships,	178-179
Renewal,	140, 141
Repeal,	141, 144, 177

INDEX TO GUIDE AND COMMENTARY

	PAGE
Requests,	142
for information,	133, 134
to read papers,	134
Rescind,	140, 141, 143, 144, 177
Resignation,	144

Resolutions [see *Motions*].

Robert, General (states),	131, 141, 147
Robert's Rules of Order (quoted),	138, 182
Rotation,	181
Rules,	144, 168
Standing,	147, 158
Suspension of,	134, 143, 144
Violation of,	162
Secretary, corresponding,	160
Executive,	152
Financial,	161
Recording,	152, 160, 162, 164, 173, 178, 180, 181
Seriatim (Consideration by paragraph),	134, 153
Signature,	159, 160, 161
Sine die,	154
Social functions,	179-180
Speakers,	168-169, 180
Take from table,	137, 140, 142, 143, 144, 154
Tally sheet,	172-173
Tellers' report,	172
Ticket,	154
Treasurer,	159-160, 161, 163, 165

Trustees [see *Board of Directors*].

Vice-President,	159, 160, 172, 177, 180, 181-182
Vote, Voting,	132, 134, 136, 138, 139, 140, 143, 145-146, 154, 159, 163, 172, 180, 181
Aye and no,	145, 163, 164

Vote, Voting *continued.*

    Majority, ...147, 153, 158, 167, 173, 176, 183
    Minority, ...157-158
    Methods, ...145
    Rising, ...145
    Roll call, ...145, 160
    Two-thirds, ...132, 136, 141, 143-144, 145, 146,
                                  154, 164, 167, 176, 180, 183
    Viva voce, ...145, 154

Yield, ...154, 161

NOTES

NOTES

NOTES

NOTES